SPENDING WISELY

Sensible Finances For Busy People

About the Author

ANTHONY SWEENEY is an independent investment analyst. A native of Limerick, he received his MBA from Edinburgh Business School at Heriot-Watt University. An expert on European financial markets, he currently resides in Germany. His previous books include *Irrational Exuberance* (Blackhall Publishing, 1999).

Spending Wisely

Sensible Finances For Busy People

ANTHONY SWEENEY

BLACKHALL
Publishing

This book was typeset by
Gough Typesetting Services for
BLACKHALL PUBLISHING
8 Priory Hall, Stillorgan
Co. Dublin
Ireland

e-mail: blackhall@eircom.net
www.blackhallpublishing.com

ISBN: 1 842180 16 9

A catalogue record for this book
is available from the British Library.

Printed in Ireland by
ColourBooks Ltd

For Togora

Contents

Introduction

The function of this book is to teach you how to use money wisely, and by so doing save a larger part of what you earn for other productive uses. Using money wisely means that:

- you control your money, not the other way round.
- you don't waste money.
- you don't get into burdensome debt.
- you have long-term plans for your money.

No matter what the current state of your finances, this book aims to assist you in achieving the above four goals with the minimum amount of disruption to your current lifestyle. You can think of this book as a financial tool-box. Some people will benefit from having a financial tune-up and learning many cost-saving strategies, while others may need a major overhaul because they are drowning in a financial mess.

This book is aimed at individuals *not* income brackets. It is often thought that those with larger incomes must be more prudent financiers than those on lower incomes. This is wrong. The more you earn, the more you have to play around with and the more trouble you can sometimes get yourself into. So whether you earn £50,000 a year or £10,000 this book will benefit you.

This book is *not* a technical manual on tax, pensions, savings, shares, or the like. There are many books out there that will drown you with details but may not address the human side of finance, nor why people behave in certain ways. Detail must be balanced with discussion as there is not much point in having twenty different saving options thrown at you if you don't understand why you should be saving. Equally there is little point in being told to 'get out of debt' if you don't understand why you are there in the first place.

While personal finances are obviously a serious topic, I have written this book in as relaxed a style as possible. I think we all spend too much time in our day-to-day lives reading turgid prose, which you can feel slowly tightening your arteries. Reading should be as enjoyable and relaxing as possible, otherwise the reader will simply put the book down. So, if you are currently standing in a bookstore and you have read this far, then might I suggest that you take the plunge and buy the book? I firmly believe that the information contained within these covers will save you the price many times over; so you have nothing to lose and much to gain.

Layout of the Book

The more I read, the more I realise that the layout of a book is critical to the value that a reader can extract from it. Each reader is different. The challenge in writing this book is trying to cater to a broad range of people without losing focus on what is important to individuals; this is a very difficult peak to scale, but I hope I have succeeded.

With the above in mind, you can use this book in a number of different ways. You can start at section I and work your way through to the end. This should allow you to obtain the maximum value from the book. It will allow you to define your own financial goals, decide where you are now, and then demonstrate how to bridge these two points. Alternatively, you might decide that you really want to jump into the meat of the book and begin at section II. This should allow you to extract many cost-saving strategies and advice without doing much self-analysis. Finally, you can just cherry pick any chapter or topic you want and extract what you will. Ideally I would go for the 'full service' option, but each to their own.

SECTION 1

Chapter 1

WHERE IT ALL BEGAN

My grandmother, I am told, would receive her husband's wages on a Friday. She would spend what was necessary and allocate the rest into a collection of jam jars, which she had on the top shelf of a wooden dresser. Each jar represented a different item for which expenditure would be due at some stage in the future. Some of the jars would receive money every Friday, others only on alternate weeks or every month. The jars had a range of titles from clothing to Christmas to doctor.

The system was simple but extremely effective and it performed many functions with the drop of a few coins and the odd paper note. As she deposited the various amounts into the different jars, she not only provided for expected future expenses, but also for the unexpected ones. In a time of no social welfare, no easy credit and very little money, she achieved a level of certainty and stability for her family. When expected, and unexpected, household bills became due, or a visit to the doctor was necessary, she was ready. My father also informs me that with a half-second glance at the top of the dresser, my grandmother could firmly establish the state of the family finances; and also whether his requested trip to the local cinema was on the cards.

Now let's zip forward to today and ask such questions. How many people reading this book really know their actual net-worth, or the true state of their finances? How many people can honestly say that they do not wonder sometimes about their long-term financial security? How many people reading this worry about money, about juggling payments for various loans and credit cards, about what is going to come in the post tomorrow? How many people, even those who are 'financially comfortable', would like to achieve something similar to the peace-of-mind and certainty my grandmother had?

Most people in today's fast-paced economies live lives that are not conducive to something known as peace-of-mind. We are running on a treadmill of earning, spending, borrowing, owing, earning, (and around and around again). We have so many different financial tentacles stretching into the machinery of banking and finance that we rarely, if ever, know our true financial worth. Whether we are financially solvent or not, many of us are getting mangled in a world where we find it difficult to control our finances and act prudently. We seem to earn money only to fritter it away on buying things we do not really want. Or worse still, we borrow money to buy these things and those 'easy payments' soon become quite difficult. Yet in most quarters of the popular media such a lifestyle seems to be celebrated. The glossy magazines sing like the sirens of Greek mythology as they lure us into danger. Advertisements and articles seem to blend together to inform, even lecture, the reader on how to achieve lifestyles that no one ever seems to achieve. Silly articles about what's in the handbags of famous women, or the fridge's of eligible bachelors, merely serve to berate the reader on their lack of the correct 'things'. Saving or investing appears about as fashionable as woolly vests and mittens (not that I am advocating either mind you).

So how did we get from my Grandmother's jars to indebted people buying expensive wine with maxed-out credit cards because they think it will make them 'more appealing'? Well, it was a simple process that will only take a moment to explain. But before I do, I should make one important point. I am *not* romanticising any bygone era, nor longing for it to return. My parents and their parents lived in tough times, which I have no interest in ever experiencing. I just want to extract some of its ingredients and try to apply them to our own lifestyle. I do like the luxuries of modern life. I am not a Luddite; I just like to be in control of my own life. What this book is aiming towards is allowing us all to experience modern life without the commensurate financial pressure. A modern consumer lifestyle can be enjoyed without feeling dread that your next month's credit card bill will arrive before (and be larger than) your salary.

Now back to history. What moved the situation from that which our fore-fathers and foremothers experienced, to the current frenzied climate? The answer is easy – money.

At the end of the last century, a small elite class of people held most of the money. They controlled most of the land and means of production, and hence they drew rents from the vast majority of people who toiled on the land and in factories. Through a long series of social and economic changes, brought about in large part by both World Wars, life slowly began to alter for many people.

Greater democracy, less monarchy, emancipation and education all cata-lysed to move western democracies towards real meritocracies. And with fair reward for fair effort, came the redistribution of income. As the money cas-caded down from the upper-classes to the now broadening middle-classes, so did the interest of those who wanted a share of that money i.e. commerce and industry. This resulted in titanic shifts in who industry catered for. The ma-jority of car production, to take one example, moved from hand producing the Rolls Royce, to mass producing family cars like the VW Beetle and the Ford Escort.

Banks and retailers soon followed with products designed to appeal to millions of potential new customers. Those with the foresight to see what was coming were handsomely rewarded. Retail enterprises who recognised that larger sales would compensate them for lower profits per sale, moved from behind their counters and opened larger retail stores. Those who didn't recognise what was occurring mostly withered on the vine. For every successful mega-supermarket, there are probably a hundred businesses that didn't change with the times and were wiped out. The most dangerous affliction for any retailer over the last three decades has been stagnancy. Darwinian theory applied brutally and it produced efficient modern retail organisations. It was a case of sink or swim.

Consumer banking and finance followed swiftly in the wake of retailing. The need for larger sales created the need for credit to finance these purchases. Simple hire-purchase plans became the thin edge of the wedge, followed by credit cards, tailored term-loans, overdrafts, store cards, leasing and so on. While consumers now had greater freedom and power to spend, it also meant that this included the freedom to paint themselves into a corner. Without delving too much into philosophy (mostly because it is all extremely boring), freedom and responsibility rise commensurately. So every time our freedom expands, so must our skills to deal with it.

In the last ten years, social and economic changes have occurred at an even quicker pace. And while this has given immense amounts of personal freedom, it has also enabled more people to get themselves into a mess. Fairy-tale lives presented in the media as reality have also increased pressure on certain people to live lifestyles that can test their financial juggling skills. To take one example, when women's liberation started at the beginning of the century it was concerned with allowing women the right to vote and live independent lives by pursuing their own careers. These rights were long fought for and were basic human rights which no rational individual could deny any person. But the unfortunate flip side is that as women entered the workforce, they drove down the price of certain labour, resulting in lower-paid jobs. The result is that it is now extremely difficult for many homes to survive on one income and hence in the case of most modern couples, women *have to work*, even after having children. This places some women under the tremendous pressure of balancing the natural maternal desires to care for their offspring with the financial pressures of modern living that now requires numerous modern appliances, pre-cooked meals, crèche expenses, two cars, mobile phones and a myriad of other items. This should not be taken as a commentary on feminism or women, just finances.

In this modern financial whirlwind, banks and retail organisations compete for our demands with financial products that can push people closer and closer to the edge. While my grandmother could look at the top shelf to figure out where she stood, the modern couple have no such luxury. There are multiple credit cards with multiple balances, there are current accounts, store cards, mortgage payments, savings accounts, term loans, shares, overdrafts, PIPs, PEPs, retirement planning, life insurance, health insurance and on and on and on. All of these have multiple options, reams of fine print and are pushed at you by slickly dressed salespeople whom you don't really trust. There are bills coming in for electricity, cable TV, gas, childcare, telephone services, health clubs (to ease the stress), car repayments, mortgages, medical services, and ten more things you didn't expect. And as the days spin by faster and faster, and money just becomes numbers on a digital display, some people cannot cope. Some slowly slip beneath the surface of it all. Without being able to focus on one item long enough to control it, they let the size of it all overwhelm them.

In many cases it is not a case of too much debt, it is a case of too little time. Too little time to properly allocate what money is coming in. Without enough time, much income that could be spent wisely is spent foolishly. I know many couples who do not owe a penny to anyone, but neither do they actually have a penny. The shortage of time and a prosperously hectic life-style deprives them of the luxury of getting off the treadmill long enough to make some long-term decisions. Many of us are short-terming ourselves to penury. But it can stop, you can gain control of it, and by controlling it, ultimately simplify it. Life *can be* easier and slower while still being comfortable.

Chapter 2

WHAT ARE YOUR GOALS?

We all have goals in life. Some are immediate: such as getting home by seven to see your favourite soap. Other goals are longer-term and involve serious lifestyle desires: such as getting a Masters and changing jobs. Some goals also alter and change with our age while others remain constant. Generally it might be said that many people's goals are in flux. The aim of this chapter is to help you clarify your short, medium, and long-term financial goals to give you a clear picture of the aims that are motivating you to read this book.

I have read many definitions as to what the difference between short, medium, and long-term is. If we are to examine these time frames in relation to your personal finances, then we should define what they are first. The best analogy I can come up with is this: when you arise in the morning, you have the long-term aim of getting to work and earning money, the medium-term goal is to navigate your way to work in your car, and the short-term goal is to get out of bed, have a shower, get dressed, have breakfast, and get into your car.

While each of these is an individual process (getting up and getting ready for, travelling to, arriving at and starting work) they are inter-linked in varying ways. While you have to arrive at work, you need not necessarily take the car. If you find that the car has broken down, then you might cycle or take the bus. And while you do not have to have a shower or eat breakfast, they generally add to your quality of life for the rest of the day. If you get up late and rush around like a headless chicken and don't eat or shower, then you are going to feel uncomfortable. On top of this, you will be stressed in the journey to work. Being stressed in traffic can lead to wasted time and energy, and more stress. If you arrive at work stressed, hungry, and not feeling fresh, then you are heading for a bad day.

To translate this into personal finances, we can see that the short-term relates not so much to a precise time-frame but to an ever-moving period of 'now' and the next few hours or days. If in the short-term you are aimless, then this means that you waste money because of lack of planning. Examples being: you don't have a monthly travel ticket so you have to waste money buying endless daily ones. Your wallet might be so stuffed with rubbish that you don't realise you have a ten pound note down at the bottom. Consequently you take twenty pounds out of the ATM, and because you have it, you spend it on ready-to-eat food. The expensive junk food is necessary because you didn't do a proper weekly shop. You didn't do a weekly shop because you were . . . and so on.

Those things may seem small matters, but they are not. They are important, they are vitally important. Such short-term financial dripping away of your money is clearly indicative of deeper problems in the medium and longer term. Many financial commentators talk in broad sweeps about retirement planning, investing in shares or whatever, but this misses the strong connection between the person who doesn't buy a cost-saving travel ticket and retirement planning for example. People who are endlessly chasing their own tail in the short-term, never focus on, or set goals for, the medium-term because they are too busy with short-term problems. There are always too many tasks to be completed in the short-term to allow you to relax with a cup of coffee and think about next month. Let's face it, if you are gunning up the car at the red lights with an overdue video on the passenger seat and have about four minutes to travel two miles before the video store closes, then you are not going to be ringing a free-phone number to ask whether you can cut 30 per cent off your car insurance, or whatever. This is the essence of medium-term goals – cost savings.

Those who are liberated from the immediate short-term concerns have those extra few minutes to climb up a bit higher and look further forward. Someone with a small amount of free time because their short-term plans are organised, has an opportunity to look at their medium-term. This might mean looking at your expenses and seeing what you can change. For example, telephone charges seem to be changing almost on a daily basis. New companies, new tariffs, new plans; we have all seen the ads in the papers and on TV. But how many people have changed companies? Not enough I am sure. In fact I am certain that a third of the people reading this could save money by switching their telephone companies for local, national, international, and internet calls. All it requires is a few minutes of time talking to the various companies by phone, and comparing roughly what you spend. If you spend £100 a month on calls, and could save just 15 per cent, then that would be fifteen pounds this month *and every month*. That's £180 a year. And looking at a ten year time frame, that would be £1,800. You can't dismiss this kind of money with a shrug. Even if you save only half of it, it is still close to £1,000 over ten years. Most of us will use a telephone over the next ten years, and you will either save the money or you won't. But if you're too busy running to pay a late bill, return a video, or fumbling with other short-term items, then you will not have time to cash in on these savings. Many large commercial concerns rely on this. They rely on what they call 'consumer inertia'; once you start paying something on a continuous basis and without any intervention they know that a large number of you will not change – no matter what savings are on offer. In fact they are fairly certain of it, no matter how much information is provided, they realise that inertia will keep their profits up with a large segment of customers. Direct debits may offer fantastic convenience for paying many bills, but they also remove the monthly ritual of actual paying. This lulls you into a false sense of security and the payment becomes something you don't really control. It is an example of how 'convenience' costs in ways that are not initially clear to most of us.

Longer-term goals are built upon the medium-term because it is the money you save from running a streamlined operation that allows you the luxury of having long-term goals. Long-term goals might be retirement at 55, or that new sports car in three years time. Whatever they are, they presuppose that you have the money to try to make them happen and the foresight to sit down and focus upon them. The money comes from setting medium-term goals and the foresight comes from the realisation that you can really save a lot of money from your day to day life – if only you did a little planning in the first place.

The person who realises that he is saving fifteen pounds a month in telephone charges also realises that he could also pick up that same phone or go online, do some research and then set up a direct debit to divert that fifteen pounds into an investment fund or savings account every month. In the space of a half-an-hour, and with a bit of research, and no more intervention, he has guided fifteen pounds from wasteful expenditure to productive use of both the money and the direct-debit facility. Although you won't believe the figures, I can assure you that if you invest fifteen pounds a month into a stock market fund over twenty years then you will have well over £10,000 at the end of it. Alternatively, if you have a twenty year £50,000 mortgage at 7 per cent you could increase your repayments by fifteen pounds a month from the start and save £4,000 in interest repayments and pay the mortgage off eighteen months earlier.

Now, most people will have read the above and probably said "wow! but that's not for me. He wants me to live like a robot, planning this, planning that. I'm not that type of person, I'm already late for work, my credit card is overdue, I have three kids and." The truth is that setting short, medium, and long-term financial goals is liberating. It does not increase the workload, it reduces it. It frees time at every step and saves money as well. 'Money makes money' is an old expression but it is true, and I might also add my own corollary of that 'time makes time'. The more time and money you can free up, the more you can make and it multiples from there on.

However, the true value of setting goals, especially long-term goals, does not come exclusively from the direct financial payoff. While it is obviously important that you save money, the money itself pales into insignificance when you look at the psychological impact on a person. A person who has goals and a general target in life:

- walks a little taller and a little straighter.

- feels a little smarter and a more self-confident.

- feels more in control of their own money.

- most importantly, wants more control.

It is the feeling of control that generates more financial benefits. Because once someone achieves a small victory, they desire more – success breeds success. For a number of people, it is important to become dominant so that they actually understand that they control and own their own money. Without delving into too much psychobabble, many people actually do not believe that they own their own money. It sounds silly I know, but many people rarely physically handle cash any more. They receive little electronic additions to their bank account. Many people see the ebbing and flowing of these little digits on paper, or on a little green screen, and to some degree become removed from it. On a certain level they see their role merely as channelling or allocating these digits, not actually keeping them. By planning, controlling and issuing instructions on a more frequent basis, we can begin to understand that this money is ours, it is a means of exchange of *our labour.* With each successful financial gain from exercising control, will come the desire for more. If you can save 15 per cent on your phone bill, why not look at the car insurance, health insurance, electricity, mortgage and so on? The real financial objective, and one that some people must arrive at, is understanding that the money they earn is theirs – and they should keep as much of it as is possible.

So now that we have talked about it, the next stage is to actually start setting goals for yourself. Forget everything that is around you, no matter how hectic, and spend a few minutes reading the rest of this chapter and together we can set your goals.

Setting Long-Term Goals

I started at long-term for a very important reason; if we began at setting short-term goals, then people would become drowned out by their current daily concerns. Better to look at what you really want first. So what are your real long-term goals? What, in an ideal world, would be your aims for your financial future? Let me suggest five sample goals, and they might stimulate some of your own.

- I would like to retire at 55.

- I would like to buy a boat in five years time.

- I would like to be mortgage-free in ten years time.

- I want my children to go a private school.

- I want to try to climb Mount Everest (trust me, it's expensive!).

As you can see, some of these financial goals obviously fold over into personal aims and desires, and this is the world we live in; it takes money to achieve many of the things we want. So now it's your turn. Just jot down some long-term goals. You might only have one, or you might have five. They don't need to be nicely phrased, or even a sentence. Once they mean something to you that's fine. They should be realistic, but don't be too stodgy. If you are a champion mountaineer and you actually do want to climb Everest then put down the time frame and the price.

1 _____

2 _____

3 _____

4 _____

5 _____

If you don't have a pen don't worry, just sit for a moment and formulate your goals in your mind. One word phrases are all right: 'debt-free', for example, clearly indicates your desires. You have now taken the first and most important step in your financial life. You now have an idea in which direction you want to go. So many of us, myself included, spent years walking around in circles and wandering off in certain directions only to return to the same point again.

I once read a very interesting story, which in fact I worked out to be roughly accurate. It went like this: if you save x pounds every month towards a pension from the age of 26 to 35 and then stopped, you would be in a better position than a 35 year old who started saving the same x pounds every month,[1] because he would still not have the same amount of money as you if you retired at 60! This story is either amazing or terribly frightening, depending whether you are 26 or 35. But it does illustrate the value of some long-term planning. It is however a bit idealistic as not many 26 years olds can see as far as 65. But if they could . . . .

Medium–Term Goals

We can now start the more focused work of breaking down your long-term goals into more definable chunks and doing something to convert them into reality.

---

1. This relies on you investing the money in some sort of stock market fund. Over the very long-term (20 years+) you can expect to reap approximately 10 per cent-14 per cent per annum. The secret is that after 7–10 years your money is, on average, growing by a little more than the X annual investment that you were putting in. This means it is in fact generating the equivalent of the annual contribution so it takes quite a long time for the 35 year old to catch up with you from a standing start. There are however a few catches concerning inflation, but overall it is true.

I cheated a little by getting you to write out your long-term goals, because, financially speaking, there are only really two goals you could have.

1.   I want x amount of money in y years, or months time.

2.   I want to reduce my debts to x in y amount of time.

In fact if you can boil these two into one; I want more of my money for myself. That is really it, isn't it? You want to keep more of your earnings for yourself so you can enjoy them over the long-term, not waste them in the short-term. This does not denigrate the specifics of your goals, these are important motivators that will keep you focused. But at the core you want to keep more of your income. And this is achieved by only one way – spending it more wisely, more prudently, and managing your affairs to achieve this.

So the setting of medium-term and short-term goals is in fact what the rest of this book is about. It is about liberating your income from your current bad habits so as to allow you to achieve the goals which you outlined above. However, each reader of this book is unique and your goals are unique. Some will want to save for retirement, some will want to get out from underneath burdensome debt, some will want a sports car in a couple of years. But all are essentially about generating cash.

I have left space below for five medium-term goals, and five short-term goals. As you read through chapters of the book, and depending on your circumstances, you will begin to identify these goals and you should fill them in. When you have finished the book you should have a complete list of long, medium, and short-term goals written down. The long-term ones may by their nature be slightly vague, but the medium-term will be more specific, and the short-term ones the most specific.

Just to clarify matters, a medium-term goal is a goal that helps save you money in the short-term, and a list of short-term goals is the execution of the medium-term goal. Confusing? Yes it is a little. Let's look at an example. Let's say in reading this book you decide that you are spending excessive amounts of money eating out and buying convenience foods to eat on the run. Then you might write down as a medium-term goal "I plan to prepare 75 per cent of the food that I eat." Everyone knows eating out is very expensive – even when it's cheap. A sandwich that contains just 30 pence worth of ingredients can cost you £3.00. A fancy pasta dish in a nice restaurant can cost £10.00 and contain 50 pence worth of ingredients. So the money you save every week from not buying sandwiches can be put into a glass jar and, for example, used to pay off part of your mortgage, or invested every month in a stock-market fund. The power of compounded interest is amazing. For example, an average £100,000 7 per cent, twenty year mortgage would cost you approximately £780 per month. But if you increase that payment by just fifteen pounds per month, then you will pay the mortgage off one year earlier. And if you increase the payment by £60 per month then you will finish with your mortgage well over three years sooner than normal (saving sub. This is real saving and demonstrates what a small amount of daily savings can achieve.

So the medium-term goal of cutting your eating-out bill may convert into the short-term goals of "making sure the fridge is full with the contents I need" and "getting up fifteen minutes earlier to make lunch." The short-term goal feeds, excuse the pun, the medium-term goal, which helps achieve a long-term aim of "paying down my mortgage in eighteen instead of twenty years". While I have left five spaces for each set of goals, this is only a beginning. You might find you have five long-term goals, twenty medium-term ones, and ultimately one hundred short-term goals. So expand into a separate note-book if you feel it necessary.

Generally it is important to have initiative and spin off on your own from this book if you feel it is suitable. This book is a guide, a rough-map to uncharted territory. If you think of some smarter way of doing something then go for it! My job is to hack through the thicket, yours is to build the road.

Medium-term goals

1 _____

2 _____

3 _____

4 _____

5 _____

Short-term goals

1 _____

2 _____

3 _____

4 _____

5 _____

Chapter 3

WHERE ARE YOU NOW?

This is a quick financial check-up which should help to identify how healthy, or unhealthy, your finances are. While it will be sufficient for our purposes, it is *not* designed to replace a professional analysis by an accountant.

When looking at personal finances, there are two simple strands that we have to look at. The first is financial, the second psychological. Psychological? Yes, it is important to gauge how people actually feel about their finances before looking at the actual numbers. So answer the following six simple questions:

(1) Do you feel in control of your finances?

(2) Do you worry about what bills the post will bring?

(3) Do you ever lose sleep over your finances?

(4) Do you regret not planning your life better?

(5) Do you ever wonder where all of your money goes?

(6) Do you have little to show for the last five or ten years?

If you answered yes to two or three of these, then it may be an indicator of anxiousness in relation to your finances. Anxiousness and apprehension result from a feeling of lack of control. So if you are losing sleep or worrying generally about bills, then it is a sign that you need more control in your finances (what this book is for). Most GPs would agree that a large number of patients visit them for stress-related problems. Stress is an often used, but misunderstood word. To me stress means that you feel compelled or pressured to achieve something, but you also feel that you lack the competence or resources to do so. You are forced into stretching to reach something but at the same time you feel you cannot reach it. While sorting your finances out will liberate much worry from your mind, there is also a special appendix (Appendix A) at the back of this book which discusses stress reduction. I have found that addressing the symptoms of stress itself, while also addressing its causes, can be very beneficial. So if you currently feel stressed by your finances, then take a quick trip to Appendix A.

Now back to the nitty-gritty of finances. The first requirement for examining one's finances is to gather together any relevant financial documents. Your last bank statement, your last credit card statement, your savings accounts, shares and whatever else you have concerning your finances. The road to financial freedom is honesty, so don't hide anything. Dig them all out of whatever drawer they have been shoved into.

Next we have to prepare a simple asset / liability statement see Figure 1. It sounds ominous but this just requires that you write *Assets* on the top of one half of a piece of paper and *Liabilities* on top of the other half. Next, underneath both headings you should also write *Liquid*, and about half way down the page you should write *Illiquid*. You now have four sections, Assets (liquid), Assets (illiquid), Liabilities (liquid) and Liabilities (illiquid).

Figure 1: Assets and Liabilities Statement

Liquid Assets		Liquid Liabilities	
Cash	£400	Overdraft	£1,060
Savings A/C	£800	Visa Card	£450
Telecom Shares	£900	Bills Due	£300
Prize Bonds	£300	Am. Express	£700
Assurance Policy	£500		
Total =	£2,900	Total =	£2,510
Illiquid Assets		Illiquid Liabilities	
Car	£7,000	Car Loan	£5,500
House	£120,000	Mortgage	£110,000
Boat	£3,000	Term Loan	£1,500
Total =	£130,000	Total =	£117,000
Asset Total =	£132,900	Liability Total =	£119,510
Current Worth =	£390		
Net Worth =	£13,390		

N.B. This is a fairly simple example but it demonstrates where everything goes and how the final figures are important figures are calculated.

Now start by writing down all of your liquid assets. Liquid means that they are easily converted into cash or are already cash. Credit bank balances, savings accounts, prize bonds, shares (at today's price), a cheque you might not have lodged, any pay you are owed and expect soon and finally any physical cash which you possess. In the Illiquid side of the asset equation, you should write down those assets which are not easily converted to cash, such as a house, a painting your granny left you in her will, your car, and so on. All of these must be put in at today's resale value, or the best approximation.

Be careful when putting down assets that you don't include junk, unless that junk can be realised at some value. You may have paid £1,000 for a designer coat, but unless you can sell it for some reasonable amount then don't include it. This is an exercise in reality, so be honest. In the final analy-sis the acid test is how much cash could you really expect to receive *into your hand for it.*

Next we move to liabilities. Under liquid on this side of the sheet, you should enter all debts that fall due in the next month. A credit card bill, monthly mortgage repayment, telephone bill, car repayment, etc. I realise you might not know all of these precisely, but estimate them honestly and to the best of your ability. This is not a precise scientific test, but the more accurate you can be the better.

In the illiquid column under liabilities you should now enter debts you owe but that do not fall due in the next month. Your total outstanding mort-gage balance for example, a car loan balance, a loan you owe your brother and the like.

Certain items might be tricky to allocate, but prudence should be your rule of thumb. If you are unsure whether a liability falls into liquid or illiquid, then ask yourself "could I be asked to pay this in the next month". An over-draft for example is one area of confusion, but since an overdraft can be called in immediately, I strongly suggest it goes into the liquid liabilities column, but you could put it into illiquid and make a good argument that it is unlikely you will be asked to pay it back.

You should now total the four different headings: liquid assets, illiquid assets, liquid liabilities, and illiquid liabilities. Also do an overall total for assets, and liabilities. We can now get a rough picture of the current state of your finances. It is more a snapshot of your situation now and over the next month rather than any long-term indicator but it allows you to gain a sense of your situation.

Now you will need to calculate two figures. Subtract your total liquid liabilities from your total liquid assets and this is what is known as your *current worth.* Next subtract your total liabilities from your total assets and you get what is known as your *net worth.* Both of these figures may be either positive or negative.

Positive Current Worth

This is a good start. It means that you should have enough money over the short-term to pay your out-goings. However, if your liquid assets just barely exceed your liquid liabilities then you probably should take a look at the next section. That said, you may have included something in liquid assets, such as shares, and this is not a good sign. If you have to sell shares to fund your next month's expenses then this is not good. In an ideal world you should be much stricter on yourself, your bank account balance plus any cash you hold should far exceed your potential liquid liabilities. In an ideal world your liquid assets should exceed your liquid liabilities by a factor of two or three. You need breathing space in financial matters.

Negative Current Worth

If your liquid liabilities exceed, or are close to, your liquid assets, then that means the money flowing out over the next month exceeds the money you have available to pay them. This indicates a problem. You don't have to panic, it may be a small problem, or it may be a big problem, but there is a problem. It might not immediately affect you, but living this way will ultimately lead to trouble. You should read the rest of this book carefully and focus on a serious adjustment in your finances. On the other hand, you may be what is known as 'cash poor but asset rich'. This will be discussed in the next section. If, however, there is a shortage of ready cash to pay bills over the next month, then I think you yourself will know why. Of the two of us, I can guarantee that you know a hundred times more about your finances than I do. And in the back of everyone's mind lies the truth niggling to get out.

If the situation is extremely serious, in the sense that you are literally running out of money, and robbing Peter to pay Paul from day to day then I suggest you go to the 'Emergency Room' chapter at the end of this book. It is an emergency section for people who need to start negotiating with creditors and initiating emergency actions.

Net Worth (Total Assets minus Total Liabilities)

The second comparison is to examine the overall total of the two columns. If you have subtracted your total liabilities from your total assets then you get what is known as your net worth. This is a fairly self explanatory phrase, if you have assets of £10,000 and liabilities of £6,000 then your net worth is £4,000. This is what you are worth financially. Sometimes this can be a very sobering figure. What, I've been working for ten years and I am worth only £4,000!

Negative Net Worth

You should have a positive net worth, i.e. your overall assets exceed your liabilities. If you have a negative net worth then this is not a good position, but it may not be a cause for immediate concern – it really depends on your current worth. If you have a negative current worth and a negative net worth, then you are in a bit of a mess. You should read the rest of the book carefully and apply what you read urgently.

If you have a negative net worth but a positive current worth, then this is a slightly better situation, although one that still demands attention. You should be focusing on discovering why this is. It can only be because illiquid assets exceed liquid assets. This may be explained by something like a negative equity situation. If you bought a house for a £100,000 and the market falls, your home may now only be worth £75,000, but still owe the building society £95,000. It is a problem, but only if you want to sell the house. If you can keep up repayments on the mortgage then it is probably of no major worry.

But whatever the cause, you should identify that you are in this position, and why.

Positive Net Worth

If you have a positive net worth then this is probably a good situation. It depends on how much you have and what it is composed of, but generally it is good. It is even better if you have a healthy positive net worth and positive current worth. It is quite possible, even frequent for certain people to have a positive net worth but actually have a negative current worth. This may seem a strange situation, but what it means is that you are 'asset rich, but cash poor'. You have assets but they are not in the form of cash; which is what most of us need to live from day to day. Such a dilemma is usually the preserve of elderly people who may be living in an enormous, and valuable house, but who do not have a sizeable income to survive, and are struggling. The costs of maintaining the house and buying food is far in excess of any income or savings they may have. And yet if they sold the house they might reap hundreds of thousands of pounds. However, they cannot bring themselves to do this. This is a terrible dilemma to be in, but there are some imaginative solutions to this problem and it is worth discussing three of them here as I quite sure a number of people reading this book may be experiencing a similar problem. If this situation does not apply to you then you can safely skip the next section.

Generating Cash From a House

If you own a substantial property, yet find yourself constantly pressed for cash, there are three options you might consider:

(1) Sell the house, buy a smaller house, or apartment, and live off the difference in prices. The profit on the sale of your personal residence is almost always tax-free. This can be the best solution and the most profitable, but in many cases people will have a strong sentimental attachment to their home. They may have lived in it all their lives and that is that, they will not sell. This is understandable but selling is an option to consider.

(2) Some financial companies now offer an innovative service that pays the owner of a house an income for as long as they live, and when the owner passes on then the company gets the house. This is an ingenious financial product that solves many problems in one go. The amount you receive obviously depends on the value of the house and your age, but it is well worth looking into. Most insurance agents can point you in the right direction for further information. On a humorous note, the first such transaction was arranged by a French insurance agent around 1965, when he was 38 and the client was a 68 year old retired ballerina. Forty years later the agent passed away, and the ballerina was still alive at 108, still

getting regular monthly cheques from the insurance company. You win some, you lose some I suppose.

(3) Finally, if you are up to it, sub-letting your property can be very profitable and enjoyable. In college I lived in an elderly women's home along with a botany professor and a hospital orderly. It was a fun house and the elderly women had a constant stream of people coming in and out. She enjoyed this activity and I think in the end we all became surrogate children for her. This situation was rare – not all tenants work out as well and it could have been a nightmare for the woman. But, it is worth considering the option as it can also add to security and safety.

Conclusion to Asset Statement

As it is impossible to cover every scenario, you should get a feel for your Asset & Liability statement yourself. It is important to grasp the significance of what such an analysis has revealed about the fragility or rigidity of your asset situation. If there were a few general conclusions that could be drawn from this, they would be:

(1) Realise that short-term debt, such as credit cards, overdrafts, etc. are inherently volatile. Relying on them causes problems for your finances in the long-term because they may be withdrawn quickly, especially an overdraft. Credit cards should be cleared monthly, and overdrafts should be reduced to zero – the rest of this book will hopefully give you the knowledge to achieve this. If you are worried about this, then I suggest you put this in as a long-term goal for yourself.

(2) If your current worth is just positive then you shouldn't necessarily be smiling now. Your current worth should ideally exceed your monthly salary by *at least* a factor of two. In fact you should have cash savings of at least twice your monthly take-home salary. This will allow you to endure any sudden period of unemployment or other financial emergency. Most people start down the slippery slope of financial trouble because they are unprepared to deal with the unexpected. It does of course depend on your job type, but those who are self-employed should obviously have a substantially larger 'safety net' than a civil servant that has been in the job for twenty years.

(3) If you have savings but *also* have an overdraft or credit card (an unusually common situation) then they technically cancel one another out. However, you are paying 20 per cent interest on your plastic but receiving substantially less on your savings – probably 4 per cent or less. So why not pay off the credit card with the savings, and effectively earn 20 per cent by lending money to yourself? Many people realise this, but they still prefer to have savings – just in case. I can partially understand this,

but it is a very expensive 'just in case'. That being said, don't leave
yourself short, but don't throw money away either. Finance is ultimately
about balancing varying demands.

It is now time to examine more closely your day-to-day spending. Again, I
must stress that this is not a precise science. It is impossible for one analysis
to cover all eventualities but they are good acid tests, and are usually revealing. You will need one more sheet of paper. On one side of the sheet write
Income, on the other side *Expenditure.*

Income

The first figure you should write down is the basic after-tax salary, which you
receive. Next you should write down any overtime, bonuses, or other payments from your employer that are not part of your basic salary. If you have a
partner, this should also be repeated for them. Add to this any other income
you may have, such as interest from money in the bank and share dividends.
These should then be totalled up to arrive at your *Total Household Income.*
That was the easy bit, now we move on to expenditure. See Figure 2 for an
example of this statement.

Figure 2: Income and Expenditure Statement

Normal monthly salary after tax   £1,400
Bonus/commission received   £400
Total income received for this month = £1,800

Fixed Monthly Expenditures (via Direct Debits)
Mortgage   £550
Health Insurance   £35
Satellite TV   £30
Car repayment   £110
Health Club   £25

Essentials		Non-Essentials	
Groceries	£400	Dining out	£200
Mortgage	£550	Clothes	£100
Car repayment	£110	Health Club	£25
Health Insurance	£35	Sat. TV	£30
		Socialising	£150
Total =	£1,095	Total =	£505

Total Expenditure per Month = £1,600
Percentage of total income spent (100/1800*1600) = 89%

N.B. Again this is a simple example and in reality your statement will probably run to a couple of pages, but it gets across the gist of the idea behind the statement.

Expenditure

Expenditure may be broken down in a number of ways. The first thing to do is to list all your direct debits, standing orders and other payments that come out of your bank account, including credit cards. List these under a heading of *Fixed*. These may include everything from your mortgage repayment, rent, car payment to a monthly subscription for satellite TV. If it is taken out without any intervention by you, then list it in this category. The reason I am asking you to detail these figures separately is that they may deserve a little closer attention later on and it is good to get them down on paper now.

Next you will want to write two more sub-headings, the first will be *Essentials* the next will be *Non-Essentials*. This is a separate list from the one above and you should include every expenditure, including whatever you have listed above. Under the heading Essentials, you should list what you spend on the basics every month, and when I say the basics, I mean the basics. When I did this task with my wife we both included some very exotic items which we both swore were essentials – however many were struck off by the other partner during the subsequent cross-check. Anyway, basics include grocery shopping, rent, transport, life insurance and so on. It may be difficult to put down precise figures for something like groceries, but please do try to give an accurate average figure.

In the non-essential section you can write down other regular or semi-regular monthly expenditures like eating out, holidays, clothes shopping, green fees, health club fees, and so on. It may take some time to identify these, but do think carefully about it and be honest. Look at chequebook stubs, credit card statements as these can remind you of things you may have forgotten. You can also include an amount for sundries into which you could roll together all of the small things like newspapers, cups of coffee, etc.

I realise people don't like doing this. In fact, this is probably the most difficult section of the book. People dislike having their lives dissected, I know I didn't like doing it. But it is all very worthwhile, nobody but you will see it, and this list will serve you well.

Once you have both segments compiled, you should total the Essential and Non-Essential and then add both totals to arrive at a Total figure for the month (you can do this analysis with weekly figures if you wish). If it is off slightly from reality, as I am sure it is, then it isn't the end of the world. Once we have a ballpark figure to work with then that is fine.

There are two figures, which I want to examine at this point.

(1) The percentage of total income that is spent. This is 100 divided by your

Total Household Income and multiplied by Total Expenditure. Ideally the lower this figure is, the better. If it is anywhere above 90 per cent then this is not too good, even above 80 per cent is not too comfortable. I would ideally like to see this percentage at 75 per cent or less. This means that you would have 25 per cent of your after-tax income available for saving and investing. But don't stop at 25 per cent, as your salary rises then so should your saving rate. Highly paid professionals should aim to consume no more than 50 per cent of their salaries on their monthly living expenses.

(2) You should also be alert to the composition of the income side of the equation when you are making the above calculation. If the income side of the equation is composed of a basic salary plus very large bonuses or overtime, then this should be noted. Ideally you should not rely on bonuses or other payments that are not guaranteed. It is an easy habit to come to rely on volatile bonuses or overtime which can then rapidly drain away and leave you stranded with high outgoing. There are many exceptions to this. If you have substantial incomes from interest on savings or dividends then this can be quite all right. In fact, interest on capital is probably the most stable type of income, and will usually not shift dramatically. I realise rates can change over the years, but they do tend to average out over a decade.

When you arrive here, you should now have a reasonably good idea of where you stand financially. You should have an estimation of your net worth and how much of your income you expend on a continuous basis. You have probably figured out that there is obviously a strong link between the two. Anyone with knowledge of bookkeeping can see that these two analyses are very roughly related to a Balance Sheet and Profit and Loss account. On a very simple level, if you earn £1,000 a month and you spend £800, then you should be building up savings of £200 a month, i.e. your assets should be rising every month by this amount. Conversely if you overspend every month, then you are soon going to see your liabilities rise and you will have a negative net worth.

The simple, but very important, conclusion to draw from this is that those who do not spend of all their income every month on frivolous items will build up tangible assets – usually cash or shares. And assets, by definition, should generate more money for you in the long-term. The final lesson to draw from all of this is that no matter what your result, the key to achieving your long-term goals is freeing up the largest part of salary so that you can begin to acquire assets which generate more money for you. This may be self-evident to people, but it is none the less something worth stating.

On an individual basis, you should now realise how well off, or not, you are financially. This is of limited diagnostic value unless you fully understand what this means and why. The next chapter of the book is going to examine the implications of the results of this chapter and examine consumer psychology. Then, we will move on to the core of the book, which is how to reduce expenditure – hence liberating more income to put towards your long-term goals.

Chapter 4

WHY WE ARE WHERE WE ARE

This is a very broad title with which to start a chapter but the aim is to explain why people do certain things and behave in certain ways with money. If you worked through the last chapter, you should now know approximately what your financial situation is. So before going on to attempt to remedy, or adjust your circumstances, we should examine why people act in certain ways in relation to their finances. It is vital to understand why we do certain things. If we don't then we are simply dealing with symptoms without ever looking at underlying causes.

With the last chapter in mind, I can surmise that there are, approximately, three basic types of people who are reading this book at the moment. The first, type A, will save a good portion of their salary regularly and live prudently whilst still enjoying themselves. They are generally cost-conscious but understand the value of spending some money to save money. The second, type B, enjoys their life to the fullest but spends most or all of their income. They rarely think about the future and figure it will take care of itself. They wander through life having a great time ... until they hit about 35 or 40 and then begin to realise that most of their friends are a lot better off than they are. And the last, type C, not only spend all of their income, but a little bit more as well. They have debts, which are probably growing larger as time passes on. They juggle credit cards and other forms of debt to keep afloat and ride on a roller coaster from one crisis to the next. They are ultimately heading for a big financial bang somewhere down the line, but feel helpless to do anything about it. They feel like they are running on a treadmill, but they don't know how to get off.

Assuming you have done the previous self-analysis and read the above categories, then I think you will generally know into which category you fall, and hence you should read the appropriate section below to help you get the maximum out of the rest of the book.

Type A

Congratulations on your financial well being. However, this book should still be of immense value to you. It can point out many cost savings strategies, and help you fine tune and prune your spending even further. As you are already sailing along nicely, you are in a prime position to implement these strategies with the least difficulty. You should move on to the "What Is

My Time Worth" section and then complete the book. There is sufficient information contained within for you to benefit immensely.

Type B

Life is a party, and more than likely you are at them all. You have a hectic life but financially speaking you are going nowhere. However, if you have bought this book then I trust you did so for a reason, and if you have read this far then you are concerned about something. More than likely, you are beginning to think about the future and you want to get your life a little more organised. This book is going to be of great help to you, but first you have realise that you want to change. You should have already defined some goals you want to reach, and you should be willing to make some changes. If you do so, then I can guarantee that as your financial situation improves and you begin to take control and plan for the future, then you will acquire a very strong feeling of satisfaction and financial well-being. You should continue on and read the rest of this chapter including the excuses list.

Type C

It isn't the end of the world; in fact it is the beginning. You may have the furthest to go to reach financial stability, but your satisfaction once you achieve it will be all the more. If you have bought this book, then I know you want to change and you are willing to work at it. And even if you feel you have lost control, I can assure you that this book will give you back the feeling of control over your finances (and hence possibly your life) that everyone deserves. It is all a question of steps, small steps, then larger steps, then leaps and finally bounds towards where you want to be. You can, and will, achieve it if you want to. I will not do it for you, that task belongs to you, but I will show you how. Most importantly, you should read the list of excuses below.

The Excuses we use to Rationalise Financial Imprudence

To begin with we should eliminate all of those excuses that block the road to financial freedom. Excuses are simply methods of deflecting self-criticism and pointing at someone, or something, else and saying "It's your fault, not mine!" If we blame someone, or something, else then we cannot correct the situation because we can only change our own behaviour. It all sounds a bit heavy-duty but don't worry about it, we are all human and everyone falls down somewhere in life. It's only a question of picking ourselves up and dusting ourselves down.

(1) Top of the list for excuses on why your finances are in a mess, or why we spend everything we earn, is that *"I don't earn enough"*. This is, in most

cases, a hollow argument that leans more towards self-pity than serious analysis. I am sorry to be so hard, but *it is* a self-pitying argument that must be quickly eliminated. If your spending habits are bad, then an income of £50,000 a year would never be enough. In fact, the majority of people I know who have been in serious personal financial messes are relatively wealthy professionals. You can live as good a life on a £15,000 salary as you can on a £30,000 one, if only you manage your money wisely. If you feel you are not earning enough, then there are many avenues for promotion and self-advancement in our society. Learning institutions have thrown their doors open to all and everyone, and no matter what age you are, you can improve your skills; and so improve the demand for your services and hence your income. If you feel you are not earning enough, then do something about it.

(2) *"My partner is the one who spends all of the money."* Well if this is so, then you and your partner must sit down and sort things out *together*. Quite often though, I have heard both partners blaming the other. It is no good pointing the finger at each other - a 'divided house falls'. If you are part of a couple, then both of you should read this book, and both should be involved in applying its contents.

(3) *"I have been really unlucky/unwise with money, but I am going to sort myself out very soon; but not just now because _____."* I have left the space blank because you can fill in your own excuse. Tomorrow never comes, and neither does the start of a diet, or getting to grips with your finances. You should start from today. The start will be as gentle and easy as you like, but you must start. Every step in the right direction is a step closer to somewhere better, and you wouldn't be reading this if you didn't want to be somewhere else.

(4) *"I'm young and carefree, it's the way I live. Everyone gets into debt when they are young, everyone goes wild, it's like a rite-of-passage."* Yes, but 'everyone' isn't there when the pieces have to be picked up. You may be 22 or 24, but soon you are 26, and your habits haven't changed. Then you're 28 and you want to buy a house and you can't because you don't have enough money and you realise your bank would rather lend money to an unstable South American banana republic than lend it to you. Then you have to start rowing against the tide to convince them that you are a safe-bet, when you really aren't. And then you're 40 and still living in rented accommodation and borrowing money and then. . . . You can be wild and carefree without borrowing money; debt is not a designer label.

Carrying on from the 'excuses', I will now discuss some very important psychological traits that make people behave in strange ways in relation to money.

By discussing each one, hopefully people will recognise if they have these traits (I think we all do in varying quantities), and once people recognise them, then I think they are half way to a cure.

What is My Time Worth?

I once saw a TV show in the US where they placed one of their employees at a cash register of a department store and pointed a hidden camera on him. When someone with an item for around ten dollars came up to pay for it, he said to them quietly "you know you can get that exact same item for five dollars less if you go to xyz store". He would direct them to the other store about five minutes away. Most of the customers would thank him for telling them the valuable tip and leave to purchase the item in the other shop. However when someone came to buy an item for around $100 dollars and he told him or her that they could get it for five dollars less at the other store, most ignored his advice. They basically said it was all right, "it was only five dollars". Now the question the programme raised was, why were people willing to make a short trip to save five dollars when they were spending ten dollars but not when they were spending $100. The selling price should have nothing to do with it; if you are willing to drive for five minutes to save five dollars what difference does it make how much you are spending. Surely the rationale people follow is "Is my time worth the small trip for five dollars?" Most people seemed to say yes, but it changed when they were spending more money. Why is this? The only logical conclusion I can draw is that we seem to think that the value of our time rises with the amount of money we are spending. This is illogical but obviously prevalent and it leads people into wasting money frequently. If, for example, you were buying a new car for £10,000 the dilemma would become even more pronounced as people began to say "it is only £100". In house purchases, I have seen people say, "it's only £1,000". All of your money takes you the same amount of time to earn, so there are no "only" amounts. The next time you are going to buy something, ask yourself the question, "What is my time worth?" If you figure your time is worth twenty pounds an hour, then stick to that. If you are buying a car and there is a cheaper garage thirty minutes across town and you are saving £100, then make the journey. Later on in the day, when your money scales are back in proportion you will be glad you did.

Painless Plastic

Frugality is often drummed into us as children. "Do you think money grows on trees?" was something I often heard as a child. So we often grow up feeling a little niggling guilt about spending money. For others, and me, it revolves around counting out the notes and handing them over to someone else. I feel as if I have formed a personal relationship with each note and don't want to hand it over. Fortunately, or perhaps unfortunately, credit and debit cards have removed this pain. Now it's just swish and it's all settled. No crisp notes, no counting out the money, no hassle, no pain, but this 'pain' of spending money was probably a good thing. Like physical pain it alerts you to something. I am not saying that credit cards are bad, they are an excellent tool for many consumers. But for some they simply anaesthetise pain that should not be dulled.

We should feel the little guilt pangs when we spend, it keeps us all under control. Credit cards are discussed at various other times in the book but suffice it to say at this moment, I think many people would be better off without them. According to a scientific study conducted by Discover Card in the US, the amount we spend on the average credit card transaction is higher than if we choose to use cash. This study was a little strange as it focused on the purchase of Arby's® roast-beef sandwiches, but the results are still valid and they indicated that people spent over 50 per cent more when they used credit cards rather than cash. And deep down we all know this to be true, we are all tempted (or even obliged) to spend more when using plastic.

Money Equals Success

I kept this one for last because I think it is the most important factor for a large number of people who find themselves in financial difficulty. In fact I would go as far as to state that the next couple of hundred words are the most important in this book. Our society teaches us, in many ways, that money equals success. We all equate the Mercedes, the big house, the exotic holidays, the expensive electronic appliances and so on with success in life. And there is nothing inherently wrong with this. I am an ardent capitalist and believe that such rewards motivate people to do better. The desire for prosperity has driven many entrepreneurs to create wonderful benefits for society as a whole. However, sometimes people get their wires crossed. The idea that material gains are the result of hard won, and very satisfying success, can become confused. Some people may believe that those same material goods will actually bring about either success or satisfaction. This is a destructive flaw in the thinking process that leads many people astray. Success comes from hard work and success brings, in most cases, the finer things in life. Material goods in themselves will not bring about success in the same way that you can't make eggs from omelettes. It is a one-way street. It is critical that people grasp this because our society has, in some cases, seriously distorted this message. Much of the pulp media discusses in minute detail the 'finer things in life' - without spending even a moment discussing how one should earn to achieve them. The inference is that the Armani suit or the designer handbag will in some way earn the money to pay for themselves.

SECTION II

Chapter 5

DEBT

I will start this chapter with a quote from Liam Edwards, an expert[1] who deals with the effects of excessive debt every day. He says that "the big problem is not consciously ignoring debts, but not being able to recognise that there is a problem." Now let's look at the story of Anne, using her own words.

I graduated from university at the age of 23 with an MA in German. While in college I had lived from week to week, money came in from a variety of sources; a part-time job, a grant cheque, and donations from my parents; the usual student life in other words. I spent nearly every penny I could get my hands on, I always thought money was for spending, it was just what students did.

I got a great job straightaway paying £18,000 a year. I couldn't believe it, I went from earning nothing to earning what I considered was a fortune. I opened a current account with a major bank and soon received my first chequebook and credit card. The bank sent me a glowing letter talking about a bright future and a long-term financial relationship. I felt important, I felt like a real adult, but I didn't act like one. I went crazy, I started spending all around me. My friends had credit cards and chequebooks too and we all sort of fed off each other's euphoria. We were too sophisticated to use cash, so we always used plastic. It was so easy and impressive just to put the credit card down or open up the chequebook. I spent most of what I earned and in the first six months I just managed to keep my head above water. Then I realised I could just make a minimum payment on the credit card and get by. Soon I was only making the minimum payment and the outstanding balance crept up slowly from five hundred pounds to over a thousand. But I couldn't stop. If I was depressed I spent to get that little boost, if I was happy I spent to stay happy.

In the meantime I was doing great at work, I got two quick pay rises in succession and suddenly I realised I was earning more than my father was. Then I received a big bonus at the end of the year because we had completed all of our projects. I had planned to pay off my credit card (and the overdraft that I now also had) with it. Instead I went out a put a deposit on a car and borrowed the rest. The car-repayment was 'only £39' a week, it seemed so

---

1. Liam Edwards the national co-ordinator of the Money Advice and Budgeting Service an credit counselling organisation with many offices across Ireland. This government inspired body is an excellent source of free advice on many personal financial matters.

little but with hindsight it was another straw on the camels back. I vowed to sort myself out, but routines became bad habits and bad habits became character flaws. A year later I had two credit cards and I owed close to three thousand pounds in total on them. My current account floated in and out of 'the red'. The bank charges were starting to mount, ten pounds for a bounced cheque, ten pounds for unauthorised overdraft, five pounds for something else. But I shoved it all to the back of my mind, I was successful, I was the woman I had read about in the glossy magazines with 200 pages of advertisements; I had made it!

Then I met Michael and things began to spiral downwards even faster. I wanted to impress him, and because I had such low self-esteem at this stage I felt I had to do this by spending on him, and me. I bought him an expensive watch for his birthday, and one for myself as well. I dazzled him, but the debt was mounting up. My minimum monthly repayment on my credit card was close to £200 and I was paying over 20 per cent interest on the outstanding balance. I was never any good at maths so I didn't take much notice of this, but I was beginning to realise that 20 per cent interest meant I would never get out of debt. My car was costing me about £400 a month, I don't know whatever happened to £39 a week but there were repayments, petrol, parking, insurance, tax, maintenance and on and on. I had store cards with another thousand and every month my current account sank deeper and deeper. Finally one month the injection of my salary did not pull it above zero. I wasn't sleeping at night and when I got up I could not face the bills, but I kept on trying to live the lie. The power of self-deception is amazing. Buying something new gave me a quick fix of feeling happy, of feeling like the woman I thought I was. I was young, intelligent but I could not face the future. Then one day it all fell apart.

I was in a restaurant with friends and when the bill came, I said I would put it on my card to simplify things. They all paid me the cash (which would keep me going for another week) and I handed over my card. Then I noticed the waiter quietly called me over to a small alcove of the restaurant where they had their desk. I slipped away from the table but a couple of other people had noticed what had happened. The waiter told me that my card had been declined. I tried my second card but that was also declined. It was such a final word, 'declined' – it hit me like a ton of bricks. I tried to pay by cheque but the owner was obviously on guard so he would only accept the card up to the cheque card limit. So I now had to put in much of the cash which I had just collected. When I returned to the table I realised everyone knew what had just happened. I wanted to ground to open up and swallow me. I laughed it off, but I went home and cried. The following week I turned up at the office and found that the entire firm had been bought out by a larger company and was being merged with their office in a city a couple of hundred miles away. Ten employees were going to be let go and I was one of them. It wasn't that I was a bad employee but it was just the way the chips fell. Other employees bemoaned their bad luck and started sending out CVs. The market was good and most realised that they would have another job quickly. I, on the other hand, began to panic. It was as if I turned around and saw an avalanche behind me but couldn't run.

When I got home that day, I gathered together all of the letters I hadn't opened and sat down at the kitchen table with a calculator. After adding up all of my bills, I realised I owed in excess of fifteen thousand pounds and I was paying an average of 20 per cent + interest on that. My interest payments alone were close to three hundred pounds a month, and this was without repaying the capital. I thought matters were bad, but I didn't realise they were this bad. I went to the bathroom and threw up. As I sat on the bathroom floor, I realised how alone I was. Nobody, not even my family, my best friends or my boyfriend knew how badly in debt I was. I had become adept at hiding matters and putting on a brave face. I felt trapped, I already had people threatening to take me to court and now I had lost my job to boot. I seriously contemplated suicide and was only saved by a voice on the other end of the line when I rang one of those help-lines in the telephone book. (I had always wondered who used those numbers, now I knew.) She convinced me that big as my problems were, I could overcome them. I was young and healthy and had a good education and in a year all of this could be behind me – as long as I tackled it now. She recommended I talk to a free government debt-counselling agency to give me the advice I so badly needed. I swallowed my pride and set about tackling the problem. And trust me swallowing my pride was the most difficult of all.

I received £2,000 redundancy and I used this to pay small portions off my various debts. I told my creditors that I was in financial difficulty but was working on matters aggressively. This lifted a great weight from my shoulders. It was amazing the relief that honesty brought. With some pressure off me I realised how in demand I was in the employment field and within a few days I had another job.

With the help of the budgeting agency, I started slashing my spending and took control of my money. For too long I realised I had fooled myself into thinking I was in control of my money, whereas in truth my money controlled me.

I took my car back to the garage and handed over the keys, I told them I didn't want it any more and that the repayments would be difficult for me. After negotiations, they agreed to cut my debt by over half and lower the interest rate on it. I went to my bank and told them I had problems and they treated me fairly and kindly. I expected a big ogre to tell me what a silly girl I had been, but it wasn't like that. It was tough but they were really honest with me. They rolled most of my debts into one loan and the interest rate was reduced to less than 10 per cent. Suddenly the repayments were becoming manageable. Then I cut up every single credit card, store-card, and cheque-book I had and closed the accounts. I was left with one deposit account into which my salary was lodged and from which I withdrew **cash** with an ATM card. I scrimped and scraped, I worked overtime and within sixteen months I had paid back every single creditor and reduced my bank loan to zero. On that day I celebrated and also opened a separate savings account. Now I save over 35 per cent of my salary every month and it feels good. While debt makes you feel slightly guilty, savings make you walk tall and feel good about yourself.

If it all sounds very easy, it wasn't. It was tough, really tough. I found out who my real friends were. After I turned down a few weekends away, I realised many people stopped calling me, including my boyfriend. I cried myself to sleep many a night, and had to live like a hermit for a while. But in the end I really found out who I was.

Borrowing

In Hamlet, a wealthy courtier name Polonius advised his son "neither a borrower nor a lender be". Well whatever about lending, most of us will be borrowers in our lives. But it is not an unfortunate necessity, some borrowing can be extremely productive and useful. Without borrowing commerce as we know it would not exist. However, in quite a number of cases, personal borrowing can go awry. Borrowing can be compared to fire; safely contained in a fireplace it provides beneficial light and heat. But it is equally capable of burning down the house if it is allowed to get out of control.

This chapter discusses why people borrow, what they should and should not borrow money for, and the various methods of borrowing money. It also discusses how much debt is acceptable, and what type of debt is good debt and what type is bad. This may sound a little boring, *but believe me at the centre of nearly all financial problems is badly managed debt.*

Let's first take a look at a brief explanation of borrowing. Borrowing by its nature, requires a lender. If you borrow ten pounds, then there must be a corresponding lender somewhere willing to lend you this money. But borrowing is a risky business, the borrower might not pay the money back. Hence private individuals are hesitant to lend large sums of their money to people they don't know. So if tomorrow you won £100,000 in the lottery, you would more than likely put in into a bank or building society. What in effect you are doing is, of course lending your money to the bank, the bank you rightly surmise is a very good risk. They have never refused or avoided the repayment of your money. And for good measure, the bank pays you for the use of your money, i.e. an interest rate. The bank then does what it is best at – it picks and chooses who to loan your money out to. Once it has arranged the loan, it handles all of the repayment details and chases any bad debtors. None of these tasks could be easily handled by the average individual. For its troubles, the bank charges a higher interest rate to lend out the money than it pays you. This is essentially how banks make money, they borrow from you at x per cent and they lend out at a higher y per cent. This is how they make a profit and their skill is in choosing who is good credit risk. Banks are essentially in the business of repackaging money and risk analysis.

This explains the nuts and bolts of banking and should also help you understand why banks are so cautious in lending out money. However, the most important questions for most people concerns their own borrowing. For the purpose of this section, there are two questions to be answered: "why should I borrow money?" and "from where?"

Why and Where to Borrow Money?

There are many times in our lives when we should borrow money, and conversely there are many times when we should not. What follows is my own subjective analysis, but I would think that most people would agree with me.

Borrowing is about bringing forward consumption. If you wish to borrow to buy a car, then you are 'consuming'– or gaining value from – the car sooner than you would normally. If you could not borrow the money, you would have to save up until you had the money to buy the car. The charge for bringing forward consumption is, of course, the interest rate you pay. In many cases, most people feel that the interest they pay is a reasonable cost for the extra utility[2] they enjoy from having the car when they otherwise would not. However, the interest payment is just one cost you may incur because you didn't have the cash to immediately make the purchase. Sticking with the car example, there are other costs, both monetary and psychological, that you must pay because you have chosen to 'buy' the car before you had all the money yourself:

- You may have to pay application fees or other loan costs.

- You may not get the best price because you did not have cash to use as leverage; no matter what dealers tell you, many prefer cash. Tangentially people also tend to haggle less with borrowed money because they have yet to actually earn it and do not fully appreciate its worth.

- You may have to, or feel obliged to, take out fully comprehensive insurance on the car so you can repay the loan if you write the car off in a crash. On a broader scale, lenders tend to oblige you to incur all possible costs protecting what is essentially their asset.

- Psychologically you may feel 'uneasy' about having something that you have not paid for. There *is* a difference between having possession of something and *owning* it.

---

2. Utility is a word economists use to attempt to quantify the use that someone obtains from an item.

- The repayment of any loan can add to your overall pressures if, for example, you lose your job.

As you can see from the example above, borrowing can incur costs that add to the actual price on top of interest, which you have to pay. However, on the plus side, you do have the utility of the item until you pay off the loan, and in many cases, this vastly outweighs the above costs (which is why borrowing for cars is extremely popular).

On the business side, borrowing can be the most rational thing for you to do. If for example, you are a self-employed plumber and the above car allows you the freedom to work longer or further away from your home, and this earns you more money, then borrowing money for the car might be the best investment you make.

To sum up, the question you have to ask yourself is, what extra *and* enduring utility will I obtain by borrowing to purchase this item? – be it a car or anything else. To be practical, we could change the word utility to money. In other words, what money will you save by bringing forward this purchase? So, if you are thinking of borrowing, then get out a sheet of paper and write down five ways you will save money by borrowing for this item. I would also write down five more costs the item will impose upon you – trust me they are there if you think long enough. In the car analogy, you might write down insurance, petrol, parking, motor tax and maintenance.

This is an extremely simple approach, but one which I have found to deliver the best results. By its very nature, it should highlight the fact that borrowing for certain items, which do not deliver continuing returns, may be wasteful. Such things may include weddings, entertainment, holidays, jewellery, furniture, clothes and so on. Now it could be argued in the broader sense that some of the above items provide utility because you will use them and derive varying forms of intangible benefit. For example, where are you going to sit in your new house or apartment if you do not have a sofa? Would a sofa not offer great utility by providing you with somewhere to sit? This, however, is not the question that comes into my mind. I would ask how precarious are your finances that you have moved into a new house or rented a new apartment and you do not have enough money to furnish it! It might be suggested that you scale back your accommodation costs so that you can afford some furniture to sit on.

On a related issue. If you have not paid off the *full* amount on your last credit card bill, then you should consider any use of the card from there on to be borrowing. So I would ask myself before I hand over my card, "is it right to borrow money to buy this item?" Be under no illusion – if you haven't paid your balance off last month, then you are unlikely to do so next month, hence you are borrowing for this item. Borrowing should be seen as the last resort for capital, not the first.

Where to Borrow Money?

Where you should borrow money from is really also asking the question, "How should I borrow money?" There are numerous institutions that allow you to borrow money and you will have to decide between many competing methods and offers. As this is quite a broad area, I am going to break this section into long, medium and short-term borrowing.

The term of a loan depends on your ability to make some form of manageable repayment combined with the general attitudes of the lender. So as a rule, long-term borrowing is usually for houses (such loans are usually called mortgages) which would run fifteen years and longer. Medium-term loans, usually called term loans, are for items like cars and such like. The term of these loans runs from a couple of years upwards. And finally short-term borrowing is usually covered with overdrafts, credit cards, and the like. Short-term borrowing, by its name rarely lasts more than a year (at least this is the theory anyway.) Generally speaking the shorter the term envisaged for the loan the higher the interest rate you will be charged. So the length of the loan and the interest rate are inversely proportional.

Long-Term Debt

Long-term debt for 99 per cent of people means a mortgage to buy their own home. A mortgage simply means a long-term loan secured on the property you are buying. While you will actually buy the house, the financial institution keeps the deeds to your property until you make the final repayment. They will also oblige you to take out insurance on the house, and life insurance on yourself (they can't really lose can they?).

Less than ten years ago you only had one real choice for mortgages, which were the building societies. You picked one and you saved with them until you had around a 10 per cent deposit; and then, applying strict criteria, they would decide to lend you a certain amount of money. The process was long, difficult, and expensive. There were also long lists of fees of one sort of another that always seem to drain you of every last penny. However, in the last decade things have altered radically as the mortgage business has been quickly deregulated. Today you can walk in off the street, or even pick up the phone, most banks or building societies are eager to lend you money. Most of the fees have been eradicated and some more 'exotic' mortgage products are now freely available. However, such financial freedom also brings with it the necessity to choose from a multitude of constantly shifting choices and this can cause great confusion. Sometimes I think you need a PhD in Finance just to be able to decipher the competing offers. Hopefully the next few paragraphs will ease this burden.

On the most basic level, there are only a number of simple questions that someone looking for a mortgage needs to ask a prospective building society or bank. But before that, there is one other simple choice you have to make – do you want to do the search yourself or do you want to use a mortgage broker? A mortgage broker, or mortgage advisor, is a person that does the shopping around for you and then advises on the best mortgage based on your circumstances. Their fee is usually paid by the financial institution that ultimately gets your business. Mortgage brokers are supposed to be independent and use all the information on the market to focus on getting you the best deal. But, and this is a big but, I would also do my own searching and shopping around before going near a mortgage broker. The reason is that the process of shopping around teaches you a lot about mortgages and it thus allows you to intelligently query the mortgage broker to ensure you are really getting the best deal – they might sometimes guide you in the direction of the largest commission. Also, you are going to be paying a mortgage back for fifteen, twenty or twenty five years so it is worth spending the time doing the research. If you aren't willing to spend this time then I would question how serious you are about this subject. Spending the time now can save you thousands of pounds over the lifetime of your mortgage.

So, get out a large pad of paper and ring every financial institution that advertises in the Yellow Pages and the national newspapers – conveniently most have free-phone numbers – and then ask them the questions listed below. If they say something you don't understand, ask them to explain it. Don't be pressured into agreeing to anything, just get all the information you can from them, thank them for their help and move on to the next one. Here are some of the important questions you should ask, and why you should ask them. If you feel there are any more inquiries you should be making, then add them to the list now and put the same questions to each institution.

(1) *I, and/or my partner, earn X and have Y for a deposit. How much of a loan are you willing to give us?* You obviously want to find out the size of a loan that you will be offered. You may not, even should not, take the maximum, but it just provides comparative figures.

(2) *What variable interest rate will you charge me and, more importantly, how much will that cost me per month per thousand repayment over a fixed period?* The 'per month per thousand' (PMPT) figure is vital. It is the best comparative tool you have for comparing mortgage lenders. If you are told that a mortgage will cost you £6.50 PMPT for a twenty year loan, then you can work out various monthly repayment amounts yourself without referring back to the lender. So if you wanted to borrow £75,000, it would cost you £487.50 (£6.50x75), if you wanted £85,000 (£6.50x85), it would cost you £552.50 per month in repayments. However, while the PMPT figure allows simple comparison, it should not by any means be the only comparison tool, there may be other factors specific to that building society or loan that will be important.

(3) *What fixed-rate mortgages do you offer?* The standard variable rate obviously varies with market conditions and unfortunately this means that
it usually varies upward at the wrong time (high interest rates and unemployment are causally linked). A fixed rate mortgage allows you to accept one rate at the start of the mortgage and keep that for up to five
years and sometimes beyond. While fixed rate mortgages are almost always higher than the standard variable rate mortgages; they can be worth
it. Interest rates cycle up and down over the years and with a variable
rate your repayments will ride this cycle. This can be unsettling and create difficulty for some family budgets. With a fixed-rate mortgage you
pay one rate, hence repayment, for the period you fixed. For example, a
person with a £100,000, twenty year mortgage would pay around £630
per month at 4.5 per cent, but if rates were to rise to 7.5 per cent, which
they could easily do, then this monthly repayment would rise to around
£810. This would be an unwanted surprise if you had not budgeted for it.
However, those with a fixed mortgage may have started off with, for
example, a 6 per cent rate and had been paying more initially, but if rates
rose within the fixed-rate period to 6 per cent or higher then they would
be happier. It can be a difficult choice to make; the temptation to go for a
lower repayment initially is strong, especially as there are so many other
costs associated with moving into a new home. But you should think
down the road a couple of years. Getting a fixed rate is effectively getting insurance against future rate rises and it may leave you smiling from
ear to ear in a couple of years time.

Many people seem to think that they can switch to a fixed-rate mortgage if and when rates start rising, and this is true. But, there's always a
but isn't there, you will find that once the markets sense any rise in interest rates then the rates at which fixed-rate mortgages are given out at will
also rise commensurately. You cannot have your cake and eat it. Fixed-
rates mortgages also have the disadvantage that you are truly fixed in, so
if rates start falling it can be very annoying being stuck at a higher rate.
Also, you may find that there are other strings attached – find out all of
these before you sign on the dotted line.

(4) *Is the variable interest rate you are offering me an introductory or special discount rate, and if so when will it end, will it rise, and if so, by how
much?* With more competition comes more 'sales promotions'. One of
these is 'introductory rates' or discount rate – this means that the financial institution charges you a lower rate for the first year (or some other
period) and then brings the rate up to their normal standard rate. It is very
important to ascertain from the bank or building society exactly what
kind of rate you will be paying after the 'lure rate' expires. And while
such introductory rates can be tempting, they should be treated very carefully. You may be paying a mortgage for twenty years, so the introduc-

tory rate for one year is not that important if the longer-term rate is higher or some other aspect of the mortgage is not to your liking.

Such novel aspects of mortgages are becoming more and more common. And it is important to flesh out exactly what is being offered and it's true long-term benefit. Another new feature being offered is the facility to take a few months break from repayment, or to pay eleven monthly payments instead of twelve. The idea is that you can skip one repayment for Christmas or summer holidays or over other cash-draining events. While these are innovative ideas, you should not think you are escaping anything. Interest is charged on every penny you owe a financial institution for every day you owe it – there is no escape. So if you skip payments, then you are going to pay interest for it somewhere. If you make eleven payments instead of twelve, then you will still be paying the same yearly total, only doing so over eleven months instead of twelve, or else you will be paying interest on the money you don't repay for the rest of the mortgage.

If you are offered such options, be sure to question precisely how they function; there is no such thing as a free lunch. However, they may offer you flexibility.

(5) *What extra charges will I have to pay in order to obtain the loan?* With this question, you are attempting to discover what hidden fees are charged up front with your mortgage. While not many financial institutions still charge an application fee, there may be other fees you have to pay to the building society for various services in connection with the mortgage. It is better to get these out into the open straight away. These can include life insurance, repayment insurance, surveyors' fees, legal fees, etc. It is easy to focus simply on one number like the APR or the cost PMPT but mortgages are a little more complicated than that. Several factors must be weighed up. Some financial institutions may charge you a low-rate but top up their charges by selling you 'in-house' insurance products.

While we are on the topic, I should also mention that along with fees you will have to pay the building society, there are also other fees and costs that may not have entered your calculations yet. These you will have to pay yourself and will include; solicitor, surveyor, estate agents fees, moving costs, stamp duty and so on. It is important that you sit down and quantify these precisely. One of the greatest surprises most people find when buying a house, is the extra costs associated with it that appear to come out of nowhere. It may be an old joke, but it is true that anyone who buys a house feels like a pelican because no matter which way they turn, they have a big bill in front of them. And while many financial institutions will allow you to roll some of these into the capital sum ('borrow them' in normal speak), you should still attempt to pay for them up front from your own resources. Borrowing money over twenty years to pay solicitors fees is not a good idea.

(6) *Ask if the financial institution offers different or alternative mortgages.*
There are many types of mortgages besides variable and fixed and sometimes they might suit your needs better, so they are worth investigating.
Three examples of these are *endowment mortgages, capped mortgages*
or *flexible mortgages*. Endowment mortgages cause much confusion, and
even controversy. With this type of mortgage, you pay *only* the interest
rate component of the loan and the rest of your monthly repayment[3] is
set aside and invested in the stock market for you. At the end of the
mortgage, your investment should have grown enough to repay the original capital sum. Endowment mortgages go in and out of favour because
sometimes people have a bonus awaiting them at the end of the mortgage
(because the investments did well) and sometimes they have a bill (when
the investment did poorly and is short of the amount needed to repay the
capital sum). The reasons some do well and some do poorly quite often
has little to do with the stock-market and more to do with who is investing the money for you. For this, and other reasons, endowment mortgages have generally fallen out of favour, especially recently when they
have attracted a great deal of adverse publicity. But do ask your mortgage broker about them, they are worth considering.

Capped mortgages are like regular mortgages but the interest rate is
set and capped at a predefined rate (higher than the standard variable
rate). However, the rate can fall when rates are falling, but cannot rise
above the capped rate. So if rates today are 6 per cent, then your interest
rates could fall when overall interest rates fall (just like a variable does),
but when rates rise, they are *capped* at the predefined rate. These mortgages sound ideal but there are catches involving starting rates and fees
and other little things. The devil is in the detail. But again, do ask about
them and take down the details for comparative purposes.

A flexible mortgage is just a name I have ascribed to a new hybrid of
mortgages that are starting to appear. They allow a great deal of flexibility in how your deal with your mortgage. In the extreme your current
account and your mortgage are blended into one and interest is charged
on a daily basis. So when your salary is paid into this account you are
immediately benefiting from it by reducing repayments. A normal mortgage repayment is extracted from your salary and the rest is free to spend
as normal, but until you do so you are saving interest. You are also able
to tailor and adjust that payment as you see fit. This is an extremely
sophisticated product but it does offer tremendous savings. Again a mortgage broker will fill you in on all of the current products in the market.

(7) *Ask the questions that nobody wants to ask.* These questions include
"What will happen if I lose my job?" "What happens if I am late with a

---

3. This is simplifying things slightly but it's basically what happens.

payment, what penalties will I pay?" "What is the procedure for repossessing my home if I default?" These are things you don't want to talk about when you are buying your home, which is exactly why you *should* do so. Some financial institutions that are now pressed to the bone on interest rate margins are finding other ways to extract money from customers. If your payment is only a few days late, you might find they have onerous penalty charges. *Borrow in haste; repent at leisure* so to speak. So now is the time to discover all of this, not when your payment is late and you have no way out. Ideally you want a flexible and friendly company which treats you like a customer, not a sheep to be shorn as close to the skin as possible – and by talking to people on the phone you can gauge the company fairly well. I have discovered over many phone conversations with various businesses, that there is a strong connection between how you are treated on the phone and how you will be treated as a customer. It is not a perfect causal link, but it is a good indicator. If the minute the phone is answered and before you say a word someone says "Can you please hold" and without waiting for your answer, you then hear "ding ... dong..ding..ding..ding..dong...dong.." for the next couple of minutes, then I suggest you take this as a message and take your business elsewhere. Imagine what it will be like if you have a problem that needs to be dealt with urgently.

(8) *Find out how much it costs to get out of the mortgage or payoff a substantial portion of it.* While your mortgage may be the best deal around right now, in five years time your circumstances may have changed and you may find a better deal elsewhere. So find out if there are any charges if you decide to move your mortgage. Also find out if you can adjust your repayments above the set monthly repayment. Many workers now receive yearly bonuses or other such payments, or you just may win £10,000 on the National Lottery. Whatever the source of your windfall income, you want something efficient to do with it, and quite often the best way to invest it is to pay off some of your mortgage. So ensure that you are able to increase the size of your payments without incurring a penalty. While it may seem strange that someone might not want your money, you have to look at it from their view point. You are paying a nice healthy interest rate to them in an even regular manner. They like this, it suits them – sudden large and irregular payments to financial institutions can 'upset' their systems.

(9) *Compulsory Insurance.* Discover if your mortgage lender requires you to take out certain insurance products, and if they require you to take them out specifically with them. These insurances can include general home insurance, disability/redundancy insurance, and life insurance.

Sometimes a lender's 'in house' insurance products can be substantially dearer that those on the open market. In general try to avoid being tied to the lender.

After ringing a number of building societies and other financial institutions, and asking the above questions, you will begin to build up a knowledge base concerning the mortgage situation. It is essential that you understand what you are dealing with. Neither I, nor anyone else, can replace your own full understanding of any issue. A book can guide you so far, but to be honest, it is up to you to do most of the legwork yourself. If you lack individual knowledge, then you may make very foolish commitments or let someone sell you a product that you don't want.

It is now that you should approach a mortgage brokers with your details and ask him what he thinks is available on the market for you. While such brokers are usually independent and working in your interest, you should not rely on it – which is why you should spend the time generating your own information and understanding. Importantly, ask the broker what fees he will receive from any mortgage lender and specifically *ask him the fees he receives from the financial institution he selects for you.* Then repeat the exercise by going to another broker, without of course telling him you were at the first one. These brokers are free, so you should at least have two opinions, if not three. Such sampling in all aspects of finance is essential to get a balance and eliminate bias from one particular person or institution.

So to sum up, selecting a mortgage begins with educating yourself about mortgages, and then discussing it with a number of mortgage brokers (and possibly the financial institutions themselves). By following this route, you understand what you are doing and you get a cross-section of professional advice. Most of this will cost nothing but a few hours of your time, and may save you twenty years of regret. One final point worth making is for self-employed people. Never use the same financial institution for your private home mortgage as you do for your business banking (even though this may be easy, and very tempting, to do). The reason for this is that hidden amongst all of the small print in those documents you sign, is probably a clause that allows any assets the bank holds belonging to you to be used against any debts you owe them. In the unfortunate event that your business fails and you owe the bank money, then they will have a strong card (your private house) to use against you, even if you didn't specifically put it in as security. Equally, your private mortgage may go awry (because of business problems) and this can 'crowd in' on your business at a time you might not need it. It is a problem, which only a few people will experience, but it is worth mentioning as it is a very difficult and messy situation. In short, be sure to put a fire-wall between your business and personal assets.

Medium-Term Debt

Medium-term debt usually involves borrowing money for two, three, four, or more years. Loans such as these are usually called term loans, although this really isn't very descriptive. The usual items for which people borrow over this period of time may be a car, boat, expensive electronic equipment and such like. Loans for these items tend to attract higher interest rates for various reasons. Interest rates in part are compensating lenders for the risk they are taking in lending you money. A small number of people may never repay loans and lenders must be compensated for this. Obviously they try to avoid this and through long experience, they have figured out the type of people and type of items that are most exposed to loan default. For example, people usually pay their mortgage before anything else. A house is their most important asset and they do not want to lose it. Hence interest rates for house purchases are usually lower – because default risk is lower. On the other hand, credit card and store-card debt is prone to larger default risks and maintenance costs so interest rates are higher. Sitting somewhere in the middle, are term loans for items like cars. Consequentially interest rates tend to average somewhere between the two. Now back to basics: the key points to raising medium-term finance are:

• *Compare, compare, compare.* It cannot be said enough times. Comparison is the key to better loans and cheaper rates. Examine every source of finance and see how their rates and costs differ. Don't just go for the easiest source of financing, because this is usually the most expensive. You must shop around and compare interest rates. In most cases 'shopping around' just means picking up the phone and ringing the free-phone numbers you will find in the newspapers, magazines, and on TV. Start first with the major banks and then move to those companies, which specialise in loans, such as Direct Line. While the major banks and building societies will usually give the best rates, there may be a cheaper source, namely Credit Unions. Many middle-class people seem to shy away from Credit Unions because they associate them with working class loans. But most of the Credit Unions of today offer an array of services at very reasonable prices to all segments of society and they would definitely be on my list of candidates.

• *Borrow from an institution that knows you and with whom you have a record.* If the institution knows you, then they may surmise that you are a better credit risk.

• *Compare the Annualised Percent Rate (APR) of all loans.* The APR is the true interest rate a loan will cost you. The lower the better. By law all loans must state the APR and usually the smaller the lettering the higher the APR. An institution with a competitive APR will declare it up front and in big type, a company with a very high APR will talk about repayments and have the APR in the really small print at the bottom of the ad.

• *Check if repayment/redundancy insurance is compulsory, and if so how much it is.* Sometimes this insurance is worth it, but quite often it is expensive and has many 'out clauses' for the company.

Short-Term Debt

Short-term debt is the area where many people get into serious trouble, simply because short-term debt costs so much and yet it is so easily available (these two factors are of course correlated). Short-term debt, by definition, is debt that you would expect to pay off within a year. It can take the form of overdrafts, credit cards, store cards, finance houses and the like. First I should say that it is my belief that no one should ever need to avail of short-term finance if your finances are in a stable state. So if you have, or are thinking of, availing of short-term debt, then this alone is a danger sign. That being said, the world is not a perfect place so all sources of finance should be discussed.

Overdrafts are usually, and I say this cautiously, the cheapest source of short-term credit and are also the most flexible. The caution with overdrafts is to ensure that you have pre-authorised the overdraft with your bank. If you don't authorise it, then you will probably pay a substantially higher interest rate, have your cheques bounced, and then have to pay a hefty fee to the bank for the ignominy of having someone come looking for you with a rubber cheque. Let's look at an example: Assuming you have a balance of £400 in the bank but you anticipate the need for short-term finance then you might request authorisation for a £500 overdraft. Assuming you get this, you could then write a cheque for £600, this will mean you are overdrawn by £200. But critically, interest will only be charged on the £200, not the £500, until you come back into credit. So you only pay interest on the amount you use and not the total overdraft facility you have – it is just a 'facility'. Also by having an overdraft facility in your current account, you get a better sense of your overall finances and this works in your favour sometimes. Using the above example, if you were £200 overdrawn and then received a salary payment directly into your bank account of £800, then it would put you back 'in the black' by £600 and eliminate the £200 debt without any action required by you. If that £200 had been owed on a credit card, your bank account would have looked much healthier than your actual finances were and also you would have to make a conscious effort to pay off the credit card (which you may not have done). These aren't great advantages, but it is better than nothing.

So if at all possible, use an overdraft via your current account for short-term finance by applying for an overdraft facility. If you are too embarrassed to do this in person, then do it by phone. However, there may be ways to utilise your credit or charge cards so as to receive up to 50 days free credit. If you want money for a very short period of time and know for certain that you can pay it back then ring your card provider and ask them when, and how, they start charging interest on both purchases and cash advances.[4]

Credit Cards and Store Cards

Credit cards are the greatest curse to those who manage their money badly, while at the same time being an extremely useful tool to those who manage their money well. This is one of the many cruel ironies of finance; those with money ride through the banking system without paying much in the way of charges, and those who have little, end up paying charges and penalties left right, and centre. So, the incentive is to become one of those with money instead of the terminally indebted. Credit cards are an excellent convenience, and an absolute necessity if you travel a lot,[5] they facilitate ever popular internet shopping, and can give you up to 50 days free cash flow. However, they also lure many people into burdensome debt and charge exorbitant interest rates on this amount to boot. It is just too easy to make the minimum payment one month when things are tight and let things ride. This 'ride' often becomes a slow slide into debt, and soon you are stuck in what our cousins in the US call perma-debt – a permanent state of expensive indebtedness, which you cannot get out of, but can just about, afford to keep servicing.

Using credit cards for short-term finance is dangerous because the odds are that short-term finance will become medium-term and paying 20 per cent plus for medium-term finance is crazy. If for example, you spent £200 on a credit card and just paid off a 5 per cent minimum balance every month, then it would take you over four years to pay off the debt in total and when you did, you would have paid off in excess of £400. This doubles the price of whatever you bought, so the next time you pay for something with your credit card, double the price tag as this is what you may end up paying. Does it seem so attractive now?

Such is the temptation with credit cards, that in many countries on mainland Europe incurring debt with them is effectively illegal, i.e. the payment of credit card bills is mandatory every month, and it is taken from your bank account without question. So all the credit-card company receives is the commission they charge the retailer for using their facilities, which varies between 1 and 4 per cent. While this is a fairly onerous form of credit control, it is extremely effective because when consumers know that they must pay the amount at the end of the month, they are much more sensible about using

---

4. It would be rare to find that they don't start charging straight away for cash advances.
5. The best foreign-currency rates are usually applied when converting foreign purchases with your credit card. This can save quite an amount of money if you are spending substantial sums abroad. However, be sure to get a credit card that does not apply a surcharge for foreign purchases, otherwise this eats into the advantage.

their plastic. However, in Ireland, the UK, the US and other western economies, credit card companies get the commission and if you don't clear your bill, they charge you exorbitant interest rates as well. It's a nice little double earner for them and it also raises issues of whether banks have any moral duty[6] due to the fact that the ideal situation for them is when you spend excessively and stay indebted permanently. The further in debt and the slower you are at making significant payments, then the better for them. Most in their defence will point out that many people pay off the total amount at the end of the month. But an equal, or larger number, might not.

So if you need short-term credit, then only use your credit card as a last resort. On the longer term, I might suggest either ensuring that the credit card company takes the full amount every month by direct debit from your bank account or obtaining a charge card such as American Express. A charge card is like a European credit card, you have to pay the balance off at the end of the month, and there is no other option. This obliges you to keep your spending in order. The only disadvantage with charge cards is that there can be a relatively hefty yearly fee and a lot less locations will accept the cards.

Store cards are worse – *do not get any of them.* Don't touch them with a barge pole – they offer nothing a credit card doesn't except the possibility of further indebtedness by extending your total credit-limit. The stores themselves realise this, and try to lure you in with free offers of this or that and promises of special treatment. Forget it!…find other sources of short-term credit.

Finance Houses

Finance Houses is a term which I use to cover a wide array of places such as small private loan companies to pawnbrokers, cheque cashing facilities, and beyond the legality line into loan sharks. And using the word shark is, I assure you, doing a discourtesy to the fish of the same name.

Surprisingly, and contrary to what many people might think, smaller finance houses are coming back into popularity in the US, UK, and starting to make a strong appearance in Ireland as well. Needless to say, these are some of the worst sources of finance in existence and usually charge the maximum legal limit for credit, and sometimes a lot more through various schemes. One of the most common loans they give is what is known as payday advances. You write a cheque (with a cheque guarantee card) and they promise not to present it to the bank until the end of the month or whenever you get paid into your bank account. For this, they charge you a fee – a very high one. But the fee is all profit, because they cannot lose on the deal – the guaranteed cheque will have to be honoured by the bank whether the customer gets funds

6. To be honest, I don't think they do. Once everyone knows the costs from the outset, then we are all responsible for our own actions.

into the account by the agreed date or not. All these institutions are doing is paying out cash on a post-dated cheque because their 'customer' obviously does not have sufficient funds in the bank until his salary is paid in. All I can say is that if you are at this stage of borrowing then you should read Chapter 11 straight away. You don't need to be in this position and there are many immediate remedies so head over to Chapter 11. Getting involved in these kinds of transactions is almost literally robbing Peter to pay Paul.

On the broader front, I could fill a book with the stories I have heard about the exorbitant charges involved when you move away from main-stream finance, so stick with high-street banks, building societies, Credit Unions, and the names you recognise. In nearly all cases, they will offer you a better deal.

How Much Debt is too Much and What is Bad Debt?

Let's start with "How much debt is too much debt?" This is an often-asked question to which I answer in most cases: any debt is too much. I do not like debt, and in those exceptions when it is necessary, then it should be strictly managed. So zero debt should be your aim in the long-term. However, I realise that the ideal is difficult to achieve, so some quantification of debt must be attempted. The first rule is a very broad, vague, but still reasonably important one. It is called the 'sleep test', and it goes like this. If you find yourself waking up at night-time worrying about your debts, then you definitely have too much. If you generally find debt worrying, then rapid debt reduction should be your main goal. Worry is unhealthy and different people have different levels of tolerance, so if you are uncomfortable with debt, then forget any trite formula that defines comfortable debt and reduce yours.

A more objective analysis of debt would look not at the level of debt itself, but the cost of that debt to you. And this is probably the key to how much debt is too much. Find out how much your debt repayment absorbs of your monthly income. If this figure is above 40 per cent then it is probably too much. However, you may also wish to examine how much of this debt repayment is composed of mortgage repayment and how much is composed of other repayments. Mortgages tend to be exempted from debt classifications because you are building up equity in a house and the house is probably an appreciating asset so it is productive debt. But debt is debt, and it constricts you in many ways so try to keep it below 40 per cent.

What Debt is Good Debt and What Debt is Bad Debt?

As I said above, indebtedness is not a desirable state of affairs but it may be necessary in some cases. With this in mind, the ideal debt should be:

- *Cheap*: the lower the interest rate the better. Five per cent difference in loan rates can make an enormous difference – so shop around.

- *Flexible*: you should be able to pay off as much of the debt as you want, whenever you want. Early debt repayment is a great source of savings, so make sure you can do this.

- *Unsecured*: You should avoid having to put collateral up for your debt: While collateral can reduce the interest rate sometimes, it may not be worth the risk. If your brother wants you to co-sign a loan to start a new business venture, then I suggest that risking your house as security for that loan may not be wise.

Chapter 6

THE BIG THINGS

This chapter covers the three major expense areas that most people have and indicates how they may be streamlined and reduced. These expenses are accommodation, transport, and general groceries, including food. These three categories may be an over-generalisation, but I think these are the major expenses of at least 75 per cent of the population.

Accommodation

Acquiring a mortgage was covered extensively in the last chapter, so I plan to focus on accommodation expenses from a different angle by looking at broader cost saving that homeowners and those renting apartments can follow.

After the Mortgage . . .

The mortgage, as many people have found out, is only one of the expenses the home owners face. In the rush to acquire a house many people forget that there are initial and continuous expenses that are important. These I will look at by focusing on a few points:

- *"Great we own a house but I don't know where we are going to sit"* summed up a conversation I had with a friend of mine who just bought a house. They had stretched themselves to afford the mortgage and all the associated mortgage costs only to find they were 'tapped out' when it came to actually furnishing the place. This is a common problem and it can lead to a continuous round of what I call 'the cheap furnishings vicious circle.' It goes like this. You cannot afford good carpets, curtains, furniture or appliances, so you buy the cheapest ones available and stretch your money (or worse borrow it) to furnish the entire house. It looks good for about a year then things start to go wrong, the carpet starts to wear, the washing machine starts to break down,[1] the furniture starts to suffer under normal use, and so on. You now have a house full of bad quality which will begin to need replacing over the next few years as it systematically fails or wears down. But again you are unlikely to be able to fund higher quality

---

1. Do not underestimate the cost of a single breakdown of one of your major appliances. Service engineers seem to charge more than brain surgeons and you may have to take time off work to be in when they call.

replacements and thus you are caught in a spiral, you cannot afford quality because you have to keep replacing bad quality. Even if you do finally get around to replacing the furniture, you have wasted a lot of money. The solution, or I should say my solution, is to furnish the house incrementally. If need be leave rooms or even an entire floor of the house unoccupied as you use whatever resources you have to purchase high quality, (long-lasting) furnishings. Quality will always pay off[2] in the long-term and save you money.

• *Insulate your money.* Modern homes are usually well insulated but you can always insulate a little better because it is you who is paying the heating bill not the builder. Older homes usually have woefully inadequate insulation and hence they need to be examined much more closely. Overall I won't bore you with the proven money-saving value of insulation, suffice it to say it is difficult to over-insulate a house. Most anything which an expert in your local DIY shop recommends will save you money. Also, it can only add to the value of the house.

Renting Apartments

Many people are choosing to utilise rented accommodation for longer periods of time, so it is well worthwhile focusing on this area. Saving money on rented accommodation can be boiled down to finding, moving in, and moving out.

Finding accommodation

• Decide exactly what you want – your own house or apartment, or sharing a house or apartment.

• Decide how much you want to spend in total.

• Decide which areas you would be willing to live in and ensure that you have ample public transportation nearby. Even if you have a car, public transport can save a lot of hassle and offer you an alternative.

• Your first source of locating vacancies should be the newspapers. Get them early, from outside the newspaper office if possible. The early bird definitely does catch the best worms. In a tight market, you should also investigate other sources that can save you much wasted time. These sources

---

[2.] Do not confuse 'quality' and designer labels. A Bosch washing-machine or WMF cutlery is quality, Gucci Handbags are designer labels. 'Quality' means suitability for purpose, durability and high technical specifications. And while designer labels **may** contain all of these, you are also paying a large premium for intangible criteria like exclusivity that serve little practical purpose.

include friends, company bulletin boards, notice boards in stores, and possibly advertising yourself. Quite often, a good advertisement can bring out quite a number of potential vacancies that you might otherwise not see.

- When you ring the prospective landlord, ask them all of the pertinent questions on the phone. There is no point travelling to see somewhere that doesn't want pets for example, if you own a dog. Ask first and save the travel! Speak slowly on the phone, speak conservatively (if that's possible) and tell the truth about your circumstances and what you want.

- Landlords are plagued by people not showing up to see places, so you can make a very good impression by just turning up on time, or even early. Also, dress as conservatively as possible. Many landlords are older and more conservative and they tend to make value judgements that you may not like, or may not even be legal, but they make them anyway and that's that – reality is a world a long way away from the ideal. You may be the nicest person in the world but if you have earrings in places other than your ears then take them out for a few minutes. Also be sure to bring a little notebook for jotting down details about each place – it is easy to forget.

- Look around the apartment or house closely. Look at things like the oven and the fridge, if they are clean then that is a good start. Ask about the neighbours: "are they quiet?", this always impresses landlords because it implies you are quiet. Examine the bathroom closely, same thing as the fridge – if it is clean that is a good sign of a landlord who takes care of their property. Finally ask about the rent *and any other charges*. Get everything out into the open from the start. Find out how the electricity, heat, and other bills are paid. Where is the meter? Who reads it? What is the normal amount per month? Who pays domestic charges, rates, or any other charges. Ensure that you are able to write down a figure, which is a good estimate of the total outlay that you will have to pay every month.

- Many landlords are willing to be flexible with the rent if they really like a tenant. Most landlords are more interested in having a quiet life and a property that is going to be returned to them in one piece. So if they really like you, then they may be willing to take slightly less than the going rate. Impress upon the landlord that you pay regularly, and offer to pay cash if you feel this will give you a stronger bargaining position.

- If you agree to a deal, then *get everything in writing*. It's an old joke but an accurate one, that verbal contracts aren't worth the paper they are written on. Get the conditions of the lease in writing from the start. If the landlord produces a pro-forma lease then all the better, but read it all before you sign it. Make sure what you are signing is what you agreed. Saying "but you said…" in six months time is worth nothing.

Moving In

When moving into rented accommodation, there are three important things that you should do.

- Inventory everything, and if the landlord has done this already, then double check this. I know this will take some time and it is as exciting as pairing your socks, but do it. There are certain 'fulcrum moments' in your money life and this is one of them. It is quite possible that a landlord's inventory list can accidentally include items that are not there. His inventory list may also include items that are damaged but marked down as new or perfect. I would also examine the apartment closely and write down on the inventory list any damage or excessive wear and tear you see around. Then sign and date this and keep a copy yourself. All of these things appear very fuddy-duddy, but they can save you money when you are moving out.

- Extending on the end of the last point, I would also take pictures of the place. Get a twelve or twenty-four roll of film and use it all taking pictures of each room including the kitchen and the bathroom. Taking a picture of a toilet or an oven may seem slightly strange, but do it. Most importantly, take pictures of anything worn, damaged, or out of place in any way. Be sure to get them developed in the next few days (for the date stamp on the back) and then stick them in your file or in that big box full of documents that is under your bed. The total cost of this will be less than ten pounds but it will give you a cast-iron insurance policy and a good addition to the verbal descriptions put down in the inventory list. Also, photographs include things that you may miss or not think significant at the time. This may seem like a belt & braces job but trust me it can save you tearing your hair out a year or so down the line when you are leaving. You may be moving out and the friendly landlord could turn very nasty because he believes you did XYZ. It's no good saying "but I'm sure…", a picture is worth a thousand words, and it might also be worth a returned deposit. Yes, as you have probably surmised, I have been 'burned' once or twice.

- Finally, if there are any neighbours then go say hello to them and immediately get on good terms with them. It can save a lot of hassle if you say "look, if you have any problems with noise, or this or that then come straight over and tell me". Better to get everything straight right from the start and avoid involving the landlord. Bad neighbours can be a nightmare.

Moving Out

If you are moving out of an apartment or house, you want to achieve two things – a good reference from the landlord and your deposit back. So give the landlord the required notice, tell him why you are leaving, and set a date for departure. Then get those photographs out to make sure that you haven't been too brutal on the place. It is reasonable to allow a certain amount of wear and tear, this is in effect what you are paying a portion of your rent for, but damage is not wear and tear. And if there is any damage done, then get it repaired or replaced. And make a big point of saying to the landlord "Oh I broke that salad-bowl but I bought you a new one." This gives the landlord a great sense of confidence about you, and may prevent him making a serious inspection or being too pernickety.

On the cleaning front, I suggest that you get a cleaner to do the whole place once over. You don't have to get in a professional crew, just a local cleaning lady – everyone sees at least one every day in some local environment such as a bank or at work. Offer her a reasonable payment for a couple of hours work to come and clean your place. Trust me, it will be worth your while in the long run. Also, tell the landlord you did this – again it can only work to your advantage.

If you do the above things, you will probably get your deposit back and then be sure to ask for, and get, a written reference on the spot. You might not need it now, but a reference from a landlord (with a phone number) is a big plus in further renting and can knock some money off the rent as it will push you into the 'saintly tenant' category. It's all about saving more money than it costs you. If you can spend fifty pounds to save a hundred then you have earned fifty.

Transport

We all need transport. Whether it is to get ourselves to and from work or to bring the groceries home on a Saturday morning. There are two major categories of transport – public and private. Public transport is provided by the government or private sector for the use of the public. Private transport is that which we provide, or purchase, for our own use. For this section, I am going to focus on the two vital questions everyone faces. The first is whether to own a car or not, the second is how to save money if you do own a car. In essence, these two questions are what transport issues revolve around.

Most people desire a car from a very young age. Cars for many people are seen as a step on the rung of adulthood and from there, we continue to replace them. There seems no other alternative, and in many cases there isn't. Public transport in Ireland and the UK has never reached the standard of mainland European levels, and I doubt it ever will. But for the residents of major cities, the viability of owning a car must still be examined closely. Traffic congestion and the rising costs of all aspects of motoring is really making car ownership an expensive impracticality.

Let's assume you own a mid-sized family car that costs £15,000 pounds to purchase. If the car lasts six years, then we are looking at a cost of £2,500 per year. Motor tax, insurance, parking and maintenance will tag on another £1,000. If you clock up a conservative 10,000 miles a year, then you are looking at another £1,000 for fuel. That's £4,500 per year for running a car. And this is definitely a modest family car; £4,500 after tax is closer to £6,000-£7,000 of your pre-tax salary. Now add to this the time you spend sitting in the car, looking for a parking place for it, cleaning it, and taking care that it is not stolen or damaged.

On the advantageous side, a car is great; it gives you convenience, it gives you somewhere to call your own in a hectic world, it transports you to and from work and play. Cars are great – no two ways around it. The question is, in a crowded urban environment, when cars are becoming like third feet, do the benefits outweigh the costs? Selling your car and moving to public transport may seem extreme, but some people I know have done it. They say that they save an absolute fortune. All the money that went into the tank is now in their pockets. So if the car repayment, the motor-tax, the insurance, the parking tickets, the parking fees and so on. They bought bikes and yearly travel tickets, and while it is a bit of hassle sometimes they have £5,000 more in the bank and they also dropped their health club membership because they cycled so much. It is not for everyone, but do think about getting rid of the car.

Owning a Car

If you have decided not to ditch the car for the time being, then don't worry I won't tell the Green Party. The aim now is to save you as much money as possible. The three areas where people can possibly save most money are purchase, insurance, and repairs/maintenance.

Purchasing a car can be an extremely daunting experience, I know because I went through it recently. The first question you want to ask yourself is "new, or second-hand?" – this question daunts many people. Governments put high taxes on car owners, simply because many people have to have them and this distorts the actual value. Once you have to sell that car second-hand, you cannot fully recoup all of that tax; it is paid and gone. So, in theory, a well maintained second-hand car should always be slightly better value than buying a new one. And it is the 'in theory' bit that can cause a lot of trouble. In reality, a new car comes with a guarantee, and you are certain where it has come from. In practice, many second-hand cars can have problems that you know nothing about, and unless you have a good mechanic with you when buying, then you could be sold a lemon. So as a *general* rule, I would suggest that you buy a very young second-hand car from a garage who is a dealer for that same brand. This ensures a good guarantee behind the car. But that is just my suggestion. Quite often with special deals it can make great sense to buy a new car and lock in a long guarantee so I will address both buying a new car and a second hand one.

Buying a New Car

There are so many models and so many extras, that you just don't know how to approach buying a new car. You feel submerged, almost drowned in the face of all the choices. So here are the five factors I would use in deciding which brand/model combination to go for:

- Reliability of the car – who wants to break down?

- Durability of engineering and style.

- Price.

- Model.

- The 'you' factor.

Reliability: If you buy a car then you want it to work and keep working, it's that simple. You can discover the most reliable cars by reading the frequent reports published in car buyers' magazines and books. But according to the reports I have read the most reliable cars in the last three years are Honda, Mazda, Subaru, Toyota, VW, and Mitsubishi. In fact most major brands are very reliable in the first number of years and getting more so as time goes on. However, brands that have had problems with reliability (i.e. increased break-down frequency) in some cars are Fiat, Citroen, Ford, Renault and even some 'prestigious' brands like Volvo and Saab. This is not a reason to avoid them, just do some investigation on their more recent models if you are set on buying one. To complicate things some 'bad' brands have good models and some 'good' brands have bad models. As a general rule I would stick with German and Japanese cars. It is a rough rule of thumb but statistics are firmly on your side if you stick with it.

Durability: Some cars are durable, while others aren't. Durable means not only that they last long, but that the styles look fresh. Physical durability is relatively easy to measure, just walk into a large local car park and examine each brand visually for rust, wear and tear, and general condition. Next get a publication like Parker's Car Price Guide and look at how fast a car depreciates, i.e. how much is a three, five or ten year old version of a particular model worth now (not always easy with newer models). It is a good measure of a car if people are still willing to pay a healthy portion of the new price in five years time. On the 'style' front it is a question of what you think stylish is and what appeals to you. Personally I like the BMW styles, they endure and it can be hard to tell old from new. Hard to measure, but do take it into account.

Price: The cheaper the better is the obvious advice here. But remember to look at the yearly cost not just the initial cost. Good cars last a long time, not so good cars can last a lot less and have higher maintenance costs. An extra few thousand can be well worth it to buy a reliable car with better fuel efficiency.

Model: If you have chosen a brand, then there are so many models and then options to choose from it can be very confusing finally settling on what to buy. Generally speaking look ahead and be practical is the only advice I can give you:

• A two door car might seem a good idea now but think about the practicalities; extra luggage, friends, babies, resale value, etc.

• Choose a realistic engine size, and one that your insurance company will view favourably. While '2.8XGIT++' looks great on the rear-end of the car it will drive your insurance way up. Modern engines are quite powerful and a 1.6 litre is as capable as a 2.0 litre was ten years ago.

• Consider diesel if you have a high mileage, although with the price differential between diesel and petrol almost gone it is getting harder to justify the extra price of diesels.

• Look for quality not gadgets. Budget cars packed with extras can become a car packed with extras that don't work in a few years time.

You: The final test is of course, to ask yourself do you like a car, do you like the feel of it, is it pleasing to your eye. This is a totally subjective valuation but it could also be the most important. It is, after all, you who will be driving around in the car for years to come. So take the car out for a long test drive and ensure that you like everything about it.

Another angle I will look at briefly, is why *not* to buy a car. Many people make the decision to buy cars based on some very shaky reasoning. Here are some of the things you should beware of:

• Don't buy a car because there is a special-offer and/or special trade-in deals.

• Don't buy a car because the dealer is offering low-interest loans or special 'per week/month' payment figures.

• Don't buy a car on the spur of the moment. Think about it for at least a number of days or weeks.

• Don't buy a car because it goes fast or goes from 0-60 in x seconds, or has one specific feature you always wanted.

This is not meant to preclude any car that might be included in the above categories, but you should make a reasoned analysis and then look at the bargains and features in the particular brand, which you have chosen.

Once you have decided on the brand and the model then you have to buy the car. There are now another set of decisions facing you; how should I finance the car, am I getting the best price, should I trade in or sell my own car separately?

- Financing a car in recent history was usually a case of deciding whether you funded it yourself or whether you borrowed money for it. Now there are sophisticated leasing and contract plans to consider. But for the private owner I will save you the trouble of looking at these because in my opinion practically all of these plans should be avoided. The main reason for this is that they tend to turn you into a renter of a car rather than an owner. Many plans have 'balloon payments' at the end of a number of years that really necessitate you surrendering the car to the dealer and starting all over again. If you buy a car you should *buy* it. You should *own it* yourself. If you have to borrow money for the car then so be it, but borrow the money to buy the car outright and then make your 36 or 48 equal monthly payments to repay the loan. Ownership of an asset gives you the freedom to decide how long you want to keep the car, and what you wish to do with it. Don't tie yourself into a straight jacket.

- Getting the best price involves haggling. Some people don't like to haggle, but then again if you don't you are forgoing a lot of money. If you are buying a new car off the lot and not trading in then you should at least get a discount of 5 per cent, if not 10 per cent discount, from the dealer. And you need to haggle to get this. If one dealer won't play ball then do try to shop around with other authorised dealers and if necessary go abroad if you live in the UK, to Belgium or Holland to secure the best price.

- If you have a car to trade in – then you are normally better off selling it privately. Many dealers don't want the extra hassle of selling another car. They have to service it, store it, clean it, insure it and so on. For this reason you are better off selling the car yourself. It can be worth hundreds if not thousands of pounds to do this, so don't take the easy option unless you are certain the dealer is giving you what you might expect privately. See *Selling A Second-hand Car* below.

Buying a Second-Hand Car

If you had to put down this book and never read another word, then you should leave with the advice 'Never buy a second-hand car privately unless you are a motor mechanic.' I realise I just told you to sell your car privately, but that is a different issue. You will nearly always get the best price selling your car privately rather than going with a dealer, but this still does not stop me from telling *you* never to buy privately. The reason for not buying a car privately is that the traps are just too big and too expensive for you to risk. I don't care what promises you can get from the person, or even if you know them (probably even worse), *don't buy privately.* The main reasons are:

• Dealers can pose as private sellers very easily and get away with it. They do this because the comeback you have with a private sale as opposed to dealer sale is limited.

• Unless you get a guarantee from a reputable dealer, then you are buying a very expensive pig in a poke. The car could look shiny and new, it could be glistening with a new coat of wax, it will have a shiny dash and low mileage, it could smell fresh and the engine could look great, and it still could be a death-trap. If you don't know anything about cars, then it could have been crashed and repaired, it could be a combination of many cars in one, it could be the biggest clunker in the world 'dressed up' nicely for the day, it could be anything on four wheels. It could be stolen with the best forged documents that the people who come to repossess it have seen (but they will still probably take it). Without a dealer's invoice and guarantee behind the car, then you are out on a ledge.

• The odometer could be turned back, the engine could be shot and just tuned up for the day. Unless you know what you are doing, then go to a reputable garage to buy a second-hand car. Yes, you may pay a little more, but that is life – in most matters you get what you pay for. And the higher price brings a lot more certainty in the form of a guarantee and legal enforceability. And yes, you still might buy something with a major defect, but at least you have a tangible dealer to attempt to gain redress from, rather than someone you met from a small ad.

Assuming you have identified the type of car you want and the price is equally to your liking then there are three common sense pieces of advice I can give you that should aid you in completing the task smoothly. First, assuming you have identified the car you want, bring along a mechanic to examine it before you buy it. If you don't know a mechanic then hire one from somewhere like the AA or RAC. It will cost a little, but it will be worth a lot more. Second, if possible contact the previous owner just to confirm details about the car. The dealer should assist in this and if not then find his name from the tax-book and look him up with directory enquiries. Finally, take the car for a long test-drive to see how it performs for you.

Selling a Second-Hand Car

Although it can be the worst way to buy a car it is also the best way to sell one. A dealer quite often cannot give you fair value for the car simply because he has to give the car a good service and clean it up, keep it on his lot for weeks or months (carrying the costs of doing so), and then put effort into selling it with a guarantee. So if you decide to sell your car privately there are a few things you can do to help ensure success:

- Have the car professionally cleaned by a car valeting service, which can only improve the price you will receive for it. Buyers like clean, fresh smelling cars with a new coat of wax.

- Get the car serviced and if possible, do the National Car Test or MOT if it is due soon. This allays many a buyers fears and it demonstrates your confidence in the car.

- Advertise the car first in local newspapers, free ad papers like Buy & Sell and Loot, and on public notice boards in supermarkets and the like. If you feel the car is worth it then you may choose national papers and/or car magazines. Be honest and straightforward in the advert, there is no point wasting everybody's time. If the car is seven years old then don't say five or six. Push the positive forward points definitely, but know where the line between good selling and bad lying is. Also, never give an address in an advertisement as it can only attract the 'cashless buyer' i.e. thieves and con men.

- When writing the ad use phrases like 'full service history', 'one careful owner', 'recently serviced' 'low mileage', 'car test completed recently' (assuming all of these are true of course). These are all strong phrases which have been shown to pull buyers in.

- When people call to ask about the car be sure to get their identity and phone number before setting an appointment. Bring someone else along when going for a test drive, check the driver is licensed and insured to drive your car and never hand the keys over until everyone is sitting in the car.

- If you take the price the dealer was going to offer you, and add on the cleaning and servicing, this will give you the floor price at which you can sell. You should of course aim well above this floor, but be realistic.

Be cautious of security. In your eagerness to sell, don't forget that there are crooked buyers out there. When it comes time to taking payment, *don't* take a cheque. While it may be messy dealing in large amounts of cash (and worrying for both parties), there is alternative solution if you wish. You simply agree to meet the buyer in their bank and when he draws the money out, you re-lodge it (if it is your bank also) or alternatively buy a banker's draft with it. You then hand over the tax-book, the keys and so on. This ensures that you get cash, it is not counterfeit (as the bank lodges it or accepts it for the draft), that you are not walking out of the bank with a pile of cash, and that the new buyer gets the car.

Running a Car

Many of us will not buy a car that often, but most run a car on a daily basis and there are many areas where money can be trimmed and saved. A penny earned may be a penny saved, but what can you do with a penny these days? It is better to save hundreds of pounds and some of these suggestions might just help you do that.

Maintenance

I should start out by saying that I am not a mechanic, and this is probably good as I would not be able to write this if I were one. I know nothing about engines, absolutely nothing. I know where to put the petrol, I know how to top up the oil, and after that, I only know when a car isn't working. However, this is good as it probably describes more than half of the motorists on the road, so I am in good company.

On the plus side, it is helpful to note that cars are becoming more and more reliable. Microchips now manage the engines, which increases fuel efficiency and reduces the need for things like an engine tune-up. Services however, are still necessary – cars break down and accidents do happen, so a trip to the garage will be necessary. So here is my advice on servicing/repairing your car:

- Always service the car at the intervals the manufacturers recommend. Many people tend to think that these are shortened to generate revenue for the dealers, but I don't think so. Even if they are, you cannot do any harm servicing a car too soon and you can save hefty amounts in repair bills later on. A serviced engine will last longer, run smoother and more efficiently and be less likely to break down in the middle of nowhere or on the way to the airport. And, most importantly, a service stamp on the owners' manual at the appropriate intervals will really add value to the car. Buyers love to see a full service history and so you are not just putting money in the pocket of the garage, you are ultimately putting money in your own pocket. As mentioned before, you have to spend to save sometimes.

- Most garages are good, but some are crooked. Some garages overcharge, some do work that is not necessary, some do a bad job, and some do all three. So find a good garage and stick with it. The problem can be finding the good garage in the first place. If you have never been to a garage then go back to the one you bought the car from. Another good source is a friend's recommendations. But both these need a good dash of the stick-your-toe-in attitude.

- If you are going to any garage for the first time, or even if you are not, then I recommend you follow some basic guidelines. Clearly explain what type of service you want, or exactly the nature of the problem. Get a price in advance, or tell them to contact you if they find something major. Explain to them that you will not pay for any repairs you have not specifically authorised. If you are told expensive repairs are necessary then shop around before giving your consent. Take note of anything they give you to sign when you hand the car in, you may be authorising them to do anything *they* deem necessary. When you collect the car, get an itemised bill and if you think it is excessive then complain in writing to the manager and ultimately the importer of the car that the garage sells.

• A common question to ask is whether or not to go to the authorised dealer or a private garage. The answer is that statistics show it doesn't matter. A report carried out by *Which* magazine in the UK demonstrated that good and bad service was given by both in equal measures. So let your own common sense be the judge. If you need a standard job like exhaust fitting or tyre change done then you are probably better off going to one of the major chains who specialise in such work, e.g. Kwikfit.

Running Costs

The major running cost of a car is petrol, but unfortunately the government effectively sets the price of this because close to 75 per cent of what you pay at the pump is taxes. So the price variability of each location is very limited and dictated by the local market. To add to this, the cost of travelling to buy fuel makes it inherently illogical because you use fuel to save money on buying fuel. So the only advice I can give in relation to fuel, is to find a garage that is reasonably cheap and convenient and when buying a car focus on fuel efficiency. Promotions, free give-aways, tokens and the like are attempts by the petrol companies to 'brand' a homogenous product and are best avoided. All fuel is essentially the same no matter what claims about 'special additives' are made. Petrol is petrol, and don't be lured into believing otherwise.

Insurance is probably the next largest running cost and this is an area where I feel many motorists can save money. There is competition in the market and rates change constantly so motorists must do broad sweeping searches when their insurance comes up for renewal. I suggest you write the date of your renewal on a small sticker and put it on your dash board. This way you will never forget your renewal date. About a month before it, you should start phoning the major insurance companies and insurance search agents. I am quite sure you will then improve your rate. All insurance companies are not the same, and rates can change on a frequent basis. Insurance companies like to blend various risks so while one insurance company may be looking for your category of risk, you might find at the same time that another company might not be. Use the freephone numbers and call, it can be worth hundreds of pounds, especially if you are risky.

Risky basically means young and male. If you are under 25, 27, 30 (depending on the insurance company) and male then you raise the big red flag. And there is nothing you can do to change your gender or your age so you should endeavour to convince the insurance company that you are a good driver. This can be done by taking certain motoring courses in addition to, or before, your driving exam. For those beyond the 'young male' category, these courses can be taken as well but there are also other ways to reduce your premiums. Among these, are parking in a garage, installing an immobiliser and/or alarm, and driving a car that is ranked as 'low risk'. It may be too late for some, but before you buy your car, do check with various insurance companies what they quote for insuring it. You may find that a bargain car has huge premiums, or visa-versa. It is important to remember that the cost of a car is much more that what you pay for it on day one – so check in advance.

To return to the issue of an immobiliser for a moment (and ignoring the fact that it can save you on your insurance), no car should be without one. In fact I feel so strongly about it that I think the law should mandate that every single car should be fitted with one. Immobilisers, for the uninitiated, are electronic devices that make starting the car for a thief difficult – not impossible, but difficult. Such devices will save your car more than any alarm and they are cheap. A small investment to save a bigger one. Other such anti-theft devices include steering wheel locks that quickly and easily fit around, or across, the steering wheel. Again they are not theft-proof but the average thief is lazy (they wouldn't be a thief otherwise) and once he sees this will probably move on to another car that hasn't got one.

Increasing your voluntary excess (the initial amount you pay yourself in the event of a claim) will also earn you a discount on the premium. Finally, some insurance companies give discounts for certain occupations and professions so clearly identify this to the insurer.

Groceries/Shopping

I was in the supermarket the other day and I suddenly got the feeling that if I tilted my head back and looked up that I would see a guy in a white coat with a clip board looking down at me. The feeling that I am a white mouse in someone else's maze is, I believe, a common feeling many people experience. For those of you who think I am exaggerating, the next time you are in the supermarket, you should take a good look around. Supermarkets are a small issue in the greater scheme of things but they are a microcosm of a society in which sophisticated and premeditated efforts are made to separate you from your money.

When you first walk to the door of a modern supermarket, you should listen to the music that is playing. A friend of mine in the business says that he could tell the approximate day of the week by just listening to this music. On quiet mornings at the beginning of the week, relaxing serene music is played so that we all slow down and idle just that little bit longer between the tempting shelves. As business gathers towards the end of the week, then so does the tempo of the music – which humans subconsciously react to. And as supermarkets must increase the speed at which you pass through their store in order to make way for more customers, then the beat must go up. On Friday and Saturday, the tempo has reached a crescendo as the space you are standing on is extremely valuable and they realise that the extra money you might spend by lingering is probably less than the extra money a new customer coming in the door will spend. In one chain they even resorted to playing military marching music which the management found worked like a charm as customers noticeably sped up their passage through the supermarket in response.

It is also interesting to examine the location of many of the basic items in a supermarket; the layout of these goods is far from random. Commonly purchased items such as bread, milk, meats, etc. are strategically strung out around the store so that consumers must tour the entire supermarket in order to get them. As we are led around, we are trawled past many items we do not need, but decide to buy anyway. 'Decide' of course is a relative term. Did you make a clear conscious decision that you wanted a certain item before you entered or were you induced to buy something you did not need. Did you really need that bunch of flowers, or that expensive bottle of Thai salad cream?

You will also discover that shelf space in supermarkets is 'sold' like real estate, and it is you that ends up footing the bill so this section of the book is designed to save you money during your weekly trips with some sensible advice:

- Use the two-stop method for shopping. This involves going to two different shops for your weekly shopping but overall it makes more sense. First, go to a big discount supermarket, such as Aldi and buy all of the essentials in bulk. Next go to a 'full-service' supermarket to purchase the more exotic items which you and your family desire. This system allows you to achieve low prices on essentials while still getting the wide choice. To streamline things, the discount end of the shopping could be done every two weeks or even every month as most products purchased in bulk also last a long time.

- Always make a list. I know it's boring, I know you may not want to look like your mother, but a list is the best way to organise your purchases. A list focuses your attention, stops you buying unnecessary junk, and it avoids you forgetting things. If you forget something, you will probably have to purchase it in a more expensive local environment.

- Always bring a small calculator. Supermarkets make a nice amount of profit by confusing us as much as possible. Is 62 pence for 625 grams better than 38 pence for 340 grams? A calculator can solve this and many other simple problems that you may just be too tired or busy to work out. It may only mean you save five or ten pence here and there, but that could be two or three pounds per shop and a couple of hundred pounds a year. And it also adds to the 'I'm in control' attitude that it is important to engender. In the US, it is law to display the price per 100 grams or per litre on the shelf with the actual price. And while this process has also started in the UK, I haven't seen it in Ireland yet. Such comparisons make life much simpler for the consumer.

- Buy generic products. Someone once told me that when he is sitting watching TV, he will drink the supermarket's own-brand beer i.e. generic, but when his friends come around he will get a recognised branded beer. This about sums it up. The same manufacturers who make the branded ones make most, not all, generic products. However, they realise that many people will always buy the branded product so they can safely segment the market and increase their sales (and profits), by utilising their economies of scale and producing more which lowers the per unit cost. All very confusing, but the bottom line is to try the generic product, if you are happy with it then use it, if you aren't, then go back to your brand. What do you have to lose? If the in-laws come around and you want to impress them, then that is up to you.

- Before you put anything into your shopping trolley, ask yourself if you really need it, or if you just decided to buy it because it's there. And if you are buying it because it is there, then that means you would not have bought it if it weren't. So it is unlikely you need it or really want it. Supermarkets are very clever and sophisticated marketers. They use colours, sounds and smells to attempt to lure you into buying what you don't need. Resist them and profit by it.

- Always look down before you buy anything. The shelves at eye-level usually contain the most expensive item in the category. This is because many flustered shoppers in a hurry look and grab when they see what they want. But if you look down to the floor level shelving, then quite often you will find the same product in a different, and cheaper brand.

- Never buy prepared or pre-cooked food if you have the time to cook it yourself. Salad in a bag is just about the most expensive way to purchase it, especially when you consider what is in it. The processing of food (and by this I mean the preparing, altering or cooking of it) will usually add substantially to the final cost of the product. If you actually look at the price of very basic foodstuffs such as carrots, potatoes, lettuce, rice, flour and so on, you will realise it is incredibly cheap – but when this is processed in any way, the costs soar. Quite often the value that is added may be worth it, but many times the value added is not worth the extra cost. Most of us have kitchens, which we can use to prepare food. It is enjoyable, relaxing and saves you money. Some products such as ready-made sandwiches or pre-packed salads are marketed in such a way as to appeal to the 'fast-paced' lifestyle image, which many people like to aspire to. The 'too busy getting on with life to cook food' image is a 'status' that is almost revered in modern societies and yet most of it is just smoke and mirrors. It is possible with just a small amount of organisation to make exotic salads, sandwiches and the like at around ten to twenty per cent of the cost of what you pay in supermarkets or restaurants. The only hurdle to get over is setting aside the time. You are not too busy or too important to prepare your own food, you are *too disorganised.* An average disorganised person could spend twenty or thirty pounds a week buying sandwiches, ready to eat junk and other 'foods' that you take home and shove in the microwave. This amounts to over £1,000-£1,500 per year or £2,000-£3,000 of your gross salary.

Chapter 7

THE LITTLE THINGS

Sometimes the little things in life can be as significant as the big things. It is said that big ships can be sunk by many little leaks, and so it is with your personal finances. Many little expenditures can lay waste to the best finances. This chapter is aimed at identifying those areas where small amounts of money can be wasted.

One point of advice before we start: read each topic and apply them. Many people who live hectic lives, and who spend a lot of money, think that 'little' things are insignificant, but they aren't. Those who waste £100 start by wasting ten or twenty pounds and those who waste ten pounds start by wasting one pound or less. And those who waste £100 or more will probably waste away most of their income. It is all progressive and closely knitted together. On the opposite side, those who make just one small alteration and save money will continue on the same path because they will begin to feel empowered. All aspects of your spending are part of you. Waste in one area will lead to waste in another. This is not a clarion call for miserliness, we all have to spend to enjoy our lives, but just spend wisely.

Telecommunications

This is a long word for the phone that you more than likely pick up everyday. With massive deregulation over the last number of years, call charges have fallen substantially; but people have also become very confused. There seems to be a blizzard of competing offers available for your phone needs. So how do you choose what company, plan, or scheme to go with? Well, the first point is to actually choose. *Do* make a conscious choice about which telephone company to use and do not just stay where you are because you are there. Inertia is the biggest source of profits for many businesses; if you draw only one mantra to chant from this book, let it be "inert people lose money, active people save money". That is a nice way of saying if you sit on your butt all the time, you're going nowhere.

Once you have made the decision to choose, then you actually have to choose - but how? I remember listening to one debate between two telecom companies concerning who was the cheapest. Both argued incessantly and threw figures at each other and in the end, I don't think the public were any better informed. In reality, however, there is no way any one provider can claim to be the cheapest for everyone because of the blend of services they offer. One company might be cheapest for you, but another person might find they pay more with it. So the best, and only, solution, for every person is to gather your last bill (or ideally your last three bills) and then ring the free-phone number for each provider which you see advertised everywhere these days and tell them the type and number of calls you make. Some people may make many local calls, and few international calls, while others may have a son or daughter in Australia and make a higher proportion of long distance calls. So call each of the providers, tell them your details and ask them what they would charge you. Only by doing this, will you find the cheapest. On average I would bet that at least 50 per cent of people would save money by switching to another provider.

Mobile phones are an area which we should also look at. Again there is competition and you should investigate with the different providers. You should also see if a package of fixed line and mobile could be arranged with any one provider. One bill and overall cheaper calling will simplify your life. However, a bigger question to ask might be, do I need a mobile phone? While they offer great advantages and freedom, sometimes they are an unnecessary frivolity which people are attracted to because they hook you with cheap introductory deals like phones for one pound. Only then you are drained of twenty or thirty pounds a month, every month, forever. And once they have you and your direct debit mandate (or credit card number), inertia sets in and you are unlikely to leave them. If you really need a mobile phone, then do get one. Mobile phones are great for many people, but consider it carefully and look at the five year cost. Ask yourself what this phone will cost you over the next five years, and question whether it is worth that. What else could you buy that would last five years and provide with equal or better utility?

I have found that for some businesspeople, a mobile phone can be as much of a blessing as a curse. What seems like more freedom can just be a lengthening of the chains. You can also find that subordinates might avoid making decisions when they can refer to you easily and push the responsibility further up the chain. This may appeal to your ego slightly, but the number one reason for small/medium business failure is the inability to delegate tasks. However, mobile phones do tend to be like nuclear weapons, they get theirs, so we gotta get ours.

Internet

This is as good a place as any to insert a few paragraphs on a very important topic, namely the internet. Firstly, phone calls to your internet service provider are obviously one aspect of your telecommunication package, so ensure that you are getting a competitive rate for these calls when you are picking a subscriber.

Secondly, and more importantly, the internet is one of the most innovative tools for the modern consumer. The internet has levelled the playing fields for consumers like nothing else in history. If used properly, it will not only save you substantial sums of money, but also give you extensive information sources, which can aid you in making better choices. Here's how:

There are two distinct areas of advantage to the consumer - one is called e-commerce and other I call e-information.

e-commerce

Most of the hype about the internet concerns what has become known as e-commerce, i.e. 'electronic commerce'. This means that many sellers of services and goods have set up internet sites from which you can purchase their products and services without ever leaving your desk. This allows consumers to browse, or comparison-shop very effectively, and comparison-shopping means that prices will ultimately be driven down as various retailers compete for your business. Normally when you comparison-shop, you are walking or driving from one shop to another to compare prices. With the internet, you can change sites/shops with the click of a mouse button. This removes an obstacle to efficient shopping as we all tend to be lazy and tire easily. How many times have you trudged around for a few hours comparison shopping only to end up buying one model or brand because you are so weary you couldn't be bothered any more. With e-commerce you never get tired because quite often just one site may give you the price of something from ten different suppliers.

Other savings can also be made from the fact that the retailer does not have to be located in expensive shopping districts. A sizeable part of any price in most high-street stores is paid for the ground you are standing on. For example, Amazon.com, the most prominent internet retailer in the US, is located in a warehouse in Seattle; other firms are literally located in some back wood where rent is by the acre not the square foot. The removal of these location expenses drives down the overheads which are ultimately attached to the cost of goods or services and this is then passed on to the consumer in the competitive market. Ultimately, the internet may remove the whole distribution chain as the manufacturers (it is already happening in the US) handle individual orders. If you think about it, walking into a shop to buy certain items is a waste of time and energy. A wholesaler buys an item from a factory, sells it to a retailer, who then unpacks it and puts it on a shelf. The consumer travels to the shop, and picks it off that shelf and it is packed up again and taken home.

Obviously there are certain products which are conducive to being sold on the internet and certain products which are not. Bags of flour or sugar are not going to be popular items, CDs or airline tickets are. Basically low weight and/or high value items, or services, which are non-tangible such as insurance, are ideal candidates. Therefore, the most prominent internet retailers tend to have one central location, offer massive choice to attract consumers and then ship orders by the post. This tends to be part of the formula for their success. The second half of the formula is having the ability to attract the customers who are confident and trust your name. One of the major fears with internet retailing is giving your credit card number over the internet, which superficially appears a logical fear, but in reality credit card fraud is extremely rare. In fact, VISA International in London states that it has had zero cases of fraud on commercial web sites reported to it - that's zero. To cap this, most prominent internet retailers guarantee to indemnify against any risk to your credit card anyway. And it is my understanding that they have never had to do this. While giving credit card details over an electronic network seems shaky, it isn't. Using advanced encryption technology and automatic processors, no human-being ever sees your card and so 'interception' is near impossible.

e-information

While e-commerce is definitely the trend of the future, there is another aspect of the internet, which I think can benefit internet users even more, and that is e-information. E-information represents the massive quantity of information that is available to aid consumers in making regular purchase decisions. Some of this information is available from internet e-commerce sites, while some comes from user-groups, consumer sites and the like. Let's take an example.

Last month I wanted to buy an electronic piano. There were many available in the local shops, but I just wasn't sure which one was best. I had focused on the CTK-601, but I wasn't sure, so I went to one of the major search sites on the internet www.yahoo.com (they troll through millions of 'pages' of information on other sites in seconds for you) and typed in CTK-601. Within seconds I had back about 200 links to other sites. Some of these were from Casio distributors, some from e-commerce retailers who sold that model, and some from bulletin-board type sites for keyboard users to exchange ideas. Within a couple of minutes I had all the details about the keyboard, and many comments from people who had bought it before. Some said it was good, others not so good. I could even 'post up' a question on one of these boards and I got back some very helpful replies from other people around the world who had used that piece of equipment. All of this information greatly aided me in my decision process. In the end, I received a good email from a guy in South Africa who had the same skill level as myself and he gave me some great advice on keyboards. Such efficiency in information exchange has enormous potential for the power of individual consumers, as it allows a pooling of experience, which will eliminate inefficient producers from the market.

In another example, I frequently use Amazon.co.uk, the internet bookseller, for reference purposes only. One of the main features of the Amazon site is that it allows people who read a book to rate it and add a small comment. So when you are looking at the details of the book online, you see the normal publishers blurb and such like, but you also see the reviews, good and bad, by readers. This greatly assists any book purchasing, even if it is not ultimately through Amazon.com. Information on prospective purchases is not all that is available. Using the internet, it is also possible to research consumer rights, obtain information on practices in other countries, research various investment options, research holiday options, compare prices across borders, examine medical practices and alternatives and a myriad of other activities that better inform the consumer. And the more informed the consumer becomes, the better for that consumer. Information truly is power.

Holidays and Travel

The more prosperous consumers become, the more they travel and travel is one area where substantial sums of money can be saved. The internet is again prominent in this area and sites like Travelocity.co.uk (but there are others so have a look around) puts you in control of your own flights and holidays. It puts most of the information travel agents have into your hands and allows you to directly access the *Sabre* computer system and book your own flights, hotels, car-hires and other travel components - it is a must for the frequent traveller.

On a more basic level, weekends away and 'mini-breaks' as they have become known as, are the most frequent form of travel, and money can be saved in a variety of ways if you follow a one simple rule - never do anything that a lot of other people are doing. This sounds a silly rule but it will save you a lot of money. Rooms over a bank holiday weekend can cost you twice what they will the weekend before or the weekend after. Car-hire, ferry travel, air travel, all costs substantially more during peak holiday periods. The quality and cost of your breaks can be substantially improved by just operating out of phase with others.

Other general travel tips include:

- Plan ahead, plan ahead, and plan ahead. Book a hotel or B&B before you go. It saves time, hassle and money.

- If you don't plan ahead and you want the best rate for a hotel, then don't walk up to the desk. Phone the hotel from a payphone (in the lobby, if necessary). Often you will be quoted a better rate because you are a potential customer. If you are standing at the desk looking tired, then you're a trapped customer.

- When flying, always book weeks in advance as the cheapest seats on the plane are sold first. If it is a long flight, then check in an hour ahead of the suggested time and ask for the over-wing emergency seats. These seats usually have double leg room and make for a vastly improved flying experience especially on flights of five hours and more.

Heat and Electricity

Modern homes are highly energy efficient but many of us do not live in up-to-date homes and there are always ways to improve the efficient use of heat and electricity. Investing in energy saving devices is not that sexy, but it is a good earner. Experts recommend that you can knock 20 per cent off your home energy bill by just following some simple activities. Many of these are 'do once and save forever' actions, which I equate to planting little money trees. Everything adds up, just remember that. Three or four pounds a week seems so little these days, but think in years not weeks – £150 to £200 sounds a lot more doesn't it. Here are the main energy saving tips which electricity companies recommend:

• Double glaze all windows.

• Use attic insulation 150mm thick.

• Take showers not baths.

• Use thick lined curtains.

• Put a lagging jacket on the hot water tank.

• Use Compact Fluorescent Lights wherever possible.

• Use automatic timers and thermostats to control heating.

Socialising

Socialising with friends and business colleagues is a minefield for many consumers because they feel under pressure to spend. If all of your friends are going to a restaurant then you obviously want to go along. Everyone wants to be part of the group, no one is going to say, "oh I can't afford that so I am going to go home and have some fish-fingers".

Just going to the pub can be extremely expensive. Drink prices always seem to be going up, something to eat afterwards, taxis and so on. Money runs like water when you go out and you are suddenly spending money you shouldn't. Here are a few tips on saving:

• Going out late is better than coming home early. So if you don't feel you can afford to keep up with people, then skip part of the evening by turning up late with some minor excuse.

• If it is possible, you should socialise in each other's homes. While this is impractical for younger people, once everyone has coupled-up, so to speak, then it becomes easier to go to each other's homes. Normal practices include a round-robin of cooking meals for the others. Meals cooked at home cost a small fraction of those from a restaurant - and you don't have to get up and leave when you are finished, deal with waiters or leave a tip.

• Try to suggest activities which are not as punishing on your wallet or purse. I know this may seem difficult and awkward but it doesn't have to be blatant. Mild suggestions can work extremely effectively in many wavering groups. So if everyone wants a weekend in London, try steering it towards a weekend in a less expensive spot that is probably a lot less packed and more enjoyable anyway.

• Decide how much you want to spend on socialising and keep this amount in cash. Don't use, or even bring your ATM card or credit cards when going out if you are trying to live on a budget.

Smoking

I smoked for a number of years so this is not going to be a health lecture, instead it is a money lecture. Smoking is probably the largest single waste of money known to man. If you smoke twenty a day, and I might digress here to add that I have yet to meet someone who smokes twenty a day; everyone I ask always says "I wouldn't smoke a whole pack, probably around ten or twelve", then this costs approximately £1,500 a year after tax. If you invested that £125 every month in a stock market fund, you would accumulate approximately £85,000 over a period of around twenty years. That is an inflation adjusted £85,000, i.e. in today's money. Now I know "if you gave up cigarettes" is like saying "if you won the lottery" to many people because they have tried already and failed. Well I tried and I succeeded, not because I have a stronger will, but because I used an original method which I think can be tailored and used by anybody. It's simple, and it isn't too difficult. So as not to bore non-smokers, I have detailed it in Appendix B. It is what I call the smoker's guide to giving up smoking, and I am optimistic that it will work for most people. If you smoke, give it a try and if you succeed then a huge financial windfall awaits you. If you don't, well your finances will continue to be drained by the dreaded weed.

Chapter 8

HOW TO SHOP

I can just hear most readers now "teach me how to shop? I know how to shop, that's the bloody problem!" But maybe you are not shopping, maybe you are just spending. Most people do not really know the art of shopping and hopefully I can rectify that in some small way. Shopping basically means the act of locating and purchasing what you want. However, this is becoming more and more difficult because there is so much to choose from. Consumerism has brought us choice but with that choice, can come confusion.

The average shopping trip goes like this:

John wants a new television to watch soccer matches. On Saturday, he gets in the car and heads out in search of the TV. He has seen a few ads in the paper and heard a few catchy jingles so he heads over to the TV-Mega-Land-shop. He parks the car and treks the half mile to the front door. An eighteen-year old, let's call him Frank, comes up and greets him. Frank met a girl last night, called Mary and is going to meet her again tonight. Frank is thinking about Mary. John wants a TV set. Frank wants Mary. So John gets shown a few sets as Frank runs off the blurb from the colour brochure which John could have read himself. John asks some intelligent questions. He has heard about something called Picture In Picture, whereby he can watch the main channel and watch another channel in a small box. Good for watching two soccer matches at the same time! Frank isn't sure so he starts fiddling with the demo models and looking at the remote control blankly, he presses some buttons and scans through the channels. 'Oh, she looks like Mary' he thinks to himself as he passes one channel. John gets annoyed and eventually starts looking around on his own. As he walks between the aisles of blinking TV sets, an avalanche of technical terms and features surrounds him. Flat Screen, Satellite Ready, Wide Screen, Scart Adapters, Black Screen, 28", 35", 55", Rear Projector, Digital TV, and on and on. John is smart so he decides he will try some other places. He drives around for another few hours and stops at about three different shops, both small and large, he sees more TVs, more prices, more features.

It is now lunch time, he is hungry he is tired and he walks into another shop where he meets Tom. Tom is a real salesman. Tom could sell ice to the proverbial Eskimo, in fact he once did in a convenience store in London, but that's another story. Tom sees John and knows a weary customer when he sees one. Tom has just sold 49 Sony TVs over the last month and knows that if he sells 50 he will get a big bonus. He is going to sell John a Sony no matter what. John is tired and Tom seems friendly, they have a good chat about soccer (Tom has never played a game in his life.) John feels Tom knows all about his needs, so he lets him recommend a set. John walks out of the shop with a new TV, which he isn't really sure about, but he thinks Tom wouldn't do him wrong. John gets home sets up the TV and isn't 100 per cent happy. No PIP, and he wanted a bigger screen. But Tom told him it had many other features.

A week later, John sees the TV he really wanted in another store and it costs £100 less than he paid. John isn't happy. John feels like a sucker and he's right. And just to round off the story; Tom got the bonus and Frank got Mary.

This little tale is all about the wrong ways to shop. Shopping is a process of two distinct phases. The first is identifying your needs and deciding exactly what you want, *and then* actively locating this. Deciding what you want means sitting down with a pen and pad, and writing all features or aspects you want *and why you want them.* In the case of the TV, John should have spent just a couple of minutes describing in brief points what he wanted. Writing things down may sometimes seems a bit juvenile to adults, but trust me it is a revealing exercise. Our thoughts and desires are scattered around our brains and we must set them down to solidify precisely what we are talking about.

With your 'wish list' written out, you then have a rough idea of what features you want. Next you should write out what you can afford to spend on this item. If you have a partner, you should also include them in the process so that both your needs are reflected accurately.

Now the search part of the process begins. As you saw from the last chapter, I am a strong believer in the internet and its information provision capabilities – hence, I strongly suggest that you use it to gain background information for nearly all purchases. If you have access to it at home or at work, it will only take a few minutes to get some good ideas and personal commentary or recommendations as I did with the electric piano. If you have to go to an internet café then so be it, it only costs a few pounds and the information you gather will be well worth it. If you have never used the Internet then now is as good time to start as any, it's easy, fun and will save you money. Find an internet café and go in, there are always staff who are more than eager to show you what to do.

In addition to the internet, there are a huge variety of other sources to gather information on your prospective purchase. The first would be books or magazines. There seems to be a magazine on nearly every imaginable subject now so take a quick peek in your local newsagents and/or library. Yes, this takes a little bit of time, but you either want to waste money or save it. And your purchase may be with you for five or ten years so a few hours of research is worth years of regret ("I wonder should I have bought the other one" is a terrible feeling.)

Once you have searched the internet and read a few relevant articles, you should start to come up to speed with the terminology associated with the item. Those acronyms, which seemed so mysterious will probably become second nature to you. You may also have a list of possible models or varieties that seem to suit your needs. Either way, it is now time to phone, not visit, a few retailers. So get out the Yellow Pages or Sunday newspaper and find some local retailers. Phone them up, tell them what features you want, what price you have in mind, and discuss matters with them briefly. Write down their responses, and any suggestions they may have, and then repeat this again. The more people you talk to, the more information you gather and the more fluent you become in the language surrounding your purchase. I realise that quite often many stores won't have people to talk to you but persevere – it will be worth it. The reason for ringing (or emailing) these people is to avoid the high pressure sales tactics that people can succumb to – "Oh it's the last one left, you better take it today. Some other guy is gone away to get money but that's his loss and your gain." You don't want this type of hype, you want to make a reasoned decision.

After a half-hour or so of research, most of us want to see and feel what we are going to buy so a visit to the stores is called for. Before you do so, you should now ask yourself one important question, do I really need a new item? Get a copy of one of those free ads papers such as *Buy & Sell* or *Lot* and check to see what is available second-hand. You know what you want now, you know the approximate retail prices and so quite often, you will find what you want, slightly used, but possibly at a bargain price.

While I do not recommend buying everything second-hand, there can be some true bargains in consumer items like TV, videos and the like. Anything electronic and without moving parts tends to last a long time and breakdowns are very rare nowadays. I have twice bought exactly what I was going to buy new by looking in the above magazines. In both cases, the people were being moved by their employers and were selling off the contents of their houses. I paid 50 per cent less for electrical items that were just a year old and will probably last another nine. I even got the original boxes and the manufacturers warranty card and instruction book. So before you buy new, check out the second-hand market.

If you have decided to go and buy new, then you should now be armed with the names of at least two or three models you are interested in and the lowest price you have discovered – you will also be well versed in the lingo. And even if you walk into the shop and they don't have what you precisely want, then you are on much firmer ground to make a different selection. Information is the key to shopping, I cannot repeat it enough times. Without information, you are at the mercy of salespeople whose interests may not be the same as yours.

Chapter 9

SAVING AND INVESTING

While debt brings forward consumption, saving stores up consumption for future use. And if excessive debt keeps you awake at night, then I can assure you that savings have a very soporific effect.

This chapter shows you why you should save and invest and then discusses the different methods by which you can do so. The aim of this chapter is to stimulate a desire to save, and then point you in the right general direction. For clarification, I should define the difference between saving and investing. From my point of view, saving is about storing up *cash* for future use. It is always available to you in cash form and ready to use at short notice, in a bank account for example. Investing is a more long-term practice and it usually involves the purchase of shares or the placing of money in tax-efficient vehicles that will mature at some point in the future. By their nature, such vehicles limit access in the short-term. However, for the purposes of this chapter, I will use the word *save* to cover both terms.

Reasons Why You Should Save

- On the intangible level, saving makes you a more confident person. With 'money in the bank' you tend to walk a little straighter down the street and hold your head a little higher. Like most intangible sensations, it is difficult to describe but you'll know it when you feel it.

- Savings allow you to save money on interest payments. Let's assume you want to buy a car. If you don't have the money, then you have to borrow it. Assuming that you borrowed £10,000 over five years at say 9 per cent, then your repayments would be about £210 per month. Interest over the period of the loan would be close to £2,500. Those with the cash would not only save paying this interest, but they would probably get a better price because they would be able to pay in cash.

- Not only will cash save you interest, but it can also reduce the interest rate you pay. Those taking out mortgages and some other loans will find that the larger the deposit you have, the more receptive the financial institution will be towards you. The lender makes the rational assumption that those who can build up large savings are more financially capable and that they also will have a bigger stake in the home and are less likely to want to lose it.

- Existing savings equal to about three to six months of your living expenses is considered prudent for most people. The reason for this is that life tends to throw many of us curve balls. You could suddenly find yourself out of a job or with a heavy unforeseen expense, or with a sudden opportunity. If, for example, you lost your job tomorrow, you may need time to find another job that suits you precisely. With money behind you, this task is greatly eased, but with money pressures you may be forced into taking a job which is not suitable for you.

Overall, saving is about providing a cushion for life's expected and unexpected knocks; it makes you a more independent person.

Now that you have an idea why you should save, we should move on the sticky question of how you should save. On the very basic level, you should always save – saving should be a habit you develop from this day on. It might only start with a large glass bottle into which you throw your coins, but do start.

First, let's look at a very basic principle that will serve you well; *risk and reward rise together.* What this means is that the higher the interest rate you are offered for your money, then the higher the risk to your capital it is? This does not mean that you should not seek higher rates but it is something to bear in mind. This principle is very rarely violated especially as rates climb beyond 6 to 7 per cent. If a bank is promising 5 per cent and some other financial instrument are offering you 10 per cent, then somewhere in the small print you will find that there is risk to your capital in some way or that the return is conditional in some way. This does not mean you should avoid such investments, but you should be aware of the increased risk associated with them. Anyway, let's look at some of the most basic ways of saving.

Post Office/Government Bonds

Saving in the post-office is, in effect, giving your money to the government. Your government, and most western governments in general, are considered the safest investment risks you can get. Let's face it; if the situation arises where the Irish, UK or US government defaults on its obligations, then everyone else will probably have defaulted before them. Because such investments are so safe, your return on the capital (i.e. the interest) will be relatively low, but you are at least *guaranteed* this return and your capital will always be safe. This method of saving suits the very conservative and those who wish to have absolute certainty.

Building Societies and Banks

Depositing your money in one of the large banks or building societies is nearly as safe as giving it to the government. Not only do these institutions

have huge resources, but also it is a near certainty that if they did get in
financial trouble, the government would bail them out. In the trade, such
financial institutions are considered 'too big to fail'. This of course raises a
very good point about banking. Banking is quite a risky business if you think
about it – and the more you think about it, the riskier it becomes. The reason
for this is that banks borrow money from you, the depositor, and lend it on to
others. It may sound funny to think of banks as borrowers, but this is what is
happening when you deposit your money with them. A depositor is lending
his money to the bank for which he receives an interest payment. The bank
then in turn, lends this money to another person or business at a higher rate.
The difference is their profits and it keeps everyone happy. When you think
about it, banks just repackage money and choose good candidates for loans.
In order to achieve a good return, the bank has to lend out about 90 per cent
of the money you deposit with them. It only keeps around 10 per cent to pay
the various people who come to take their money out. They know from experience that many will just leave their money in a bank, and some more will be
continually depositing so they know their average need for cash to pay back
the 'loans' from depositors.

However, the catch is that you, as a depositor, have the right to demand
your money back immediately, whereas the loans given out by the banks are
for a fixed period. This exposes the bank to the possibility of a 'run', i.e. a
rush of depositors looking to withdraw money, which the banks would not
have. In fact, I can state with near certainty that the banks have less than 10
per cent of the money they owe depositors on hand. Fortunately in most western
countries, such runs are very rare because banks are so well trusted, plus the
regulation and control surrounding them is very sophisticated. If a run does
occur on one bank, then other banks would come to its aid, and if a run
occurred on all banks, then government via the Central Banking system would
provide cash as needed – that is the theory of course.

Within the major banks and building societies, there is obviously still
some competition for your money, so it is well worthwhile shopping around
and telling the institution how much money you have. Also, you will usually
receive higher interest rates if you give up the right to withdraw your money
immediately (the reason should be clear from the above discussion) and the
longer the time period you surrender the money for, then the higher the rate
you will receive.

The Stock Market

The Stock Market is both the most over and under-hyped saving vehicle.
Many people find it all very confusing and believe it is the preserve of the
wealthy and elite. This is half right, but a broader explanation is necessary
because in the right circumstances, the stock market is the best investment
vehicle for many people. Let's go back to banking for a minute. The money

you deposit in a bank is usually pooled together and given to industry in the form of loans. These loans buy new equipment, build new factories and generally increase production and profits for the business and the wider economy. The company pays interest on these loans to the bank, and some of this is passed on to you. However, sometimes companies have bad years and sometimes loans go bad; but the bank will still continue to pay you regularly. This is because they have thousands of loans in many industries and the good balances out the bad each year. So effectively, the bank is like a shock-absorber for you, it evens out a highly cyclical return on your investment and guarantees your capital, so your return is predictable and stable *but* very low compared to what industry pays for the use of what is essentially your money. For this reason, many people wish to bypass the banks and invest their money directly with a company and get the full return. The method for doing this is to buy a share in a company (a stock is really something else, so we will just call them shares to avoid confusion.)

A share is just what it sounds like, a share of a company. If you buy one share in Cadburys, then you own a very small portion of that company and you are entitled to a very small portion of the profits they earn; this portion is known as a dividend. The price you pay for the share (the share price) changes on a continuous basis depending on the supply and demand of shares in that company at any one moment. The prices you see in the paper or on TV, are just the last price at which two people bought/sold the shares on the market. So if you wanted to invest £1,000 in Cadburys shares, you would have a broker do this for you. In return, you get a yearly dividend and your shares will, on average, increase in price as the value of the company rises. In total, the average annual return to an investor is about 10 to 14 per cent per annum. Wow! Yes wow, but there are big, big catches. Here are the main ones:

- The return is *on average,* and this is *a*, if not *the*, critical point. Share prices rise and fall in an undulating wave that usually goes upwards. But there are years, sometimes long spans of years, when a share price may fall as recessions come and go in the economy. The way around this is to invest for the long-term in a variety of shares. The absolute minimum length of time for safe stock-market investment is five to seven years and the ideal period is ten to twenty years (or even longer). The ideal spread of shares is at least ten or more.

- Most small investors are usually attracted to the stock market for all the wrong reasons and so end up losing money and never going back. Small investors get mesmerised during a period of constantly rising share prices, and after a time decide to join the party and jump in and buy shares. *Wrong!!* This is a fatal mistake because periods of rising prices are usually followed by periods of falling prices. So what happens is that small investors pile in at the top of one cycle (out of nothing more than childish greed) and when the market falls, they bail out at much lower prices out of fear.

- Small investors rarely know what shares to buy and so, quite often, buy on the basis of 'a tip' they read in the paper or heard in the pub. *Wrong!!* Unless you have unique specialist knowledge about certain industries, you should always invest via an Investment Trust, Mutual Fund, or a Unit Trust. These are very simple schemes, which are designed to allow a shareholder to invest with ease by buying a share in a larger pot of shares, which are chosen by professional managers. Such schemes are usually excellent vehicles for the small investor because all he has to do is invest his money and sit back and do nothing. No deciding when to buy or sell, no worrying about ups and downs, just letting time pass by.

- Small investors must be willing to feed money into such schemes on an annual or monthly basis. Share prices rise and fall, *nobody* really knows when 'high' is high or 'low' is low, so the ideal investor is one who can invest a fixed amount every month over the long-term and *will not need access* to this money in the short-term.

If you allow for all of the above caveats, then investing in shares is the best long-term investment vehicle for those who truly understand what is involved – and who are also calm individuals who are financially secure and not in for a quick buck. To demonstrate the amazing potential of say 12 per cent annual return versus 4 per cent, then just imagine you invested £10,000 in year X in one of the larger building societies and another £10,000 in one of the larger Investment Trusts. Twenty years later, you would have almost £22,000 in the building society, but you could reasonably expect to have £96,000 in Investment Trust shares. The growth of compounding values is incredible. Just remember the warnings, however. Investing in shares is for the very long-term, by individuals who don't need the money during the period, are financially stable, and do not lose sleep if the market falls 30 per cent or rises 30 per cent in one six month period.

Now the Practicalities . . .

This book does not attempt to address the volumes of savings and tax regulations that are currently in effect. Once you move beyond simple savings in a bank or building society, each person needs professional advice concerning the most effective and tax efficient method to save. Whilst short-term saving is easy, the longer the term becomes, the more potential for tax-savings. Such savings can boost your nest-egg substantially and should be fully availed of. Pensions, for example, are just very long-term savings. You only get out what you put in so the earlier you start the better.

Getting started, a novel savings methods (even for the wealthy!).

Start by getting a big glass bottle and throw all of your loose change into it every night. Now, many people may think this is for kids and just a glorified piggy bank. But think again. When combined with what is known as mortgage prepayment, it can lead to amazing savings (it has already become very popular in the US). Prepaying a mortgage basically means making extra repayments off the capital sum of your mortgage in addition to your standard monthly repayment.

It works like this. Every day you throw your odd coins into the large jar, pot, rubber duck or other chosen vessel. At the end of every month, or six months or whatever, you count the money and lodge it into your mortgage account (i.e. ask for it to be used to reduce the amount of mortgage capital you owe) as an extra payment on top and separate from your regular monthly payment. The money might only work out to ten pounds a week, or even less. Let's assume the worst and that both you, and your partner's loose change only comes to £25 a month. This is around 80 pence a day. If you put this against a £100,000 30 year fixed 8 per cent mortgage every month, then you will save over £23,000 in interest payment and reduce the term of the mortgage by three and a half years. *What!!* Yes, I have your attention now, don't I? The power of compounding interest is amazing. From day one every extra one pound you pay in is reducing the principle you are servicing over the loan and this stops the building society collecting interest on that pound for the rest of the mortgage. Now this is real saving, this converts your loose change into real money. If your mortgage period is lower or your interest rate is lower, then you are obviously not going to benefit by as much, but it will still be very substantial. This type of saving is relatively painless and it puts the money to good use rapidly. The most important point is that, when you are taking out the mortgage, to ensure that the building society allows prepayment, and if they don't, then do a bit of shopping around before giving up. Allowing you to take chunks regularly, or irregularly, out of your mortgage at various times means you can literally save thousands of pounds and/or years of repayment.

Now let's look at two different situations:

Jenny

Jenny didn't earn very much at her job, but she was sensible and had big plans. She was taking night classes in university and hoped to get a much better job once she qualified. Her budget was tight but she managed to save twenty pounds a week in the post office. Once she had £1,000 there, she moved it to a building society deposit account where it now earns 5 per cent. Once she finished her degree, she got a god job starting at £20,000, this was almost double her previous salary. Now she really shifted into high gear. She found that along with a better lifestyle, she could save at least £400 a month with the aim of buying her own flat. Three years later, she had close to £20,000 and her salary had now risen to £22,000. Saving had become a habit, much like brushing her teeth. She discovered that the apartment, which she had been living in, was for sale and she approached her building society for a loan. With her good job, her deposit and her saving record, she had no problem securing a loan for the apartment. So now, instead of throwing away the rent money every month, she is building up equity in her own home.

Jenny demonstrates the value of saving, no matter how little. It is the act of saving that is important, not the amount. Jenny had a plan, she wanted to get somewhere and saving was a part of that. She chose the post office initially because they had no account fees, no set up charges and didn't mind the ten or twenty pound depositor coming in. Jenny felt comfortable with them at this stage in her life. Once she reached a large enough sum, she moved it to a building society because she knew that someday she would want a mortgage and wanted to have a savings record with them. Once her income increased, her saving habit stuck with her and she saved a very healthy proportion of her income. So while the initial amounts she was saving were small, they developed the saving habit. With a larger salary, her savings then built up very quickly until she had a relatively substantial sum and could contemplate the purchase of her own home. While many building societies will offer mortgages to any reasonably sound consumer, they feel more comfortable dealing with customers who they can see have a long record of financial prudence. Being more 'comfortable' may not just mean a lower rate, it might mean allowing a larger loan, or not charging some fees. A long-term financial relationship with one institution is usually a sound financial move.

Mark and Janice

Mark and Janice are both doing quite well. Their joint income exceeds £50,000 per year and they are prudent savers. Recently they saw something on TV about investing in the stock markets. They didn't really know that much so they contacted the Association of Investment Trust Companies and the Unit Trust Investment Body; both of these bodies were featured in the TV programme. They received back various booklets, which they both read carefully. After discussing their aims, they decided to save £250 a month with a large Investment Trust. They realised that this was going to be a very long-term investment, maybe ten years or more, and that they could not rely on this money for any other commitments they had to meet. They were, metaphorically planting a grove of oak trees. They were willing to wait and they understood the risks they were taking. The money is now taken monthly from their account and they hardly feel it. The market actually fell 20 per cent in a big crash last month, but they took no notice, they are in for the long-term.

It is worth re-iterating again that the stock market is the best place to invest your money *but* it must be for the long-term and with a full understanding of what you are doing.

Chapter 10

THIRTY WAYS TO SAVE CASH

This chapter is designed to offer you thirty ways to save cash beginning immediately. It is a chapter that can be read at any time, by anyone. The advice ranges from the general to the specific, from the normal to what some might consider bizarre, but they all work and I think everyone can find at least ten pieces of advice here that will save them the cost of this book (not a bad return on your investment). Some of the information given here is already mentioned in the book (because I think they are worth repeating again) but most of the points raised are new. I should mention that this chapter is not a Misers Charter – misers never make any real money, they simply don't spend what they have. Sometimes you have to save to spend, and sometimes spend to save. The trick is knowing the difference.

Ask the price: I don't know about you, but I have found that at least 10 to 20 per cent of the items I buy are more expensive than I thought they were. This occurs for a mixture of reasons ranging from misplaced barcodes on shelves to badly designed menus. This can be quite annoying, and costly. The price of something is a vitally important component of the purchase decision. What may be a bargain at £1.99 might be a rip-off at £3.99. So I now ask the price of something if I am in any doubt – with a barcode just compare the last three digits on the item with those on the label on the shelf. It seems fairly basic but some people, myself included, are initially embarrassed at asking prices. Get over it and save some money in the process, don't be intimidated out of the practice. An addendum to this point is to be sure to get a full written estimate before any work on your behalf begins so that you can clarify and predict expenses.

Examine financial statements: I am nearly sure that if you examine your bank statements (and statements from other financial institutions), you will find mistakes in your favour. Most people just receive them and glance at the balance and then file it away in a drawer. Instead, you should get a pencil and tick each item to be sure it is correct. Also check that you are not been over-charged (or underpaid) interest. Banks are notorious for diddling people out of interest and the larger the account, the more room they have to hide. This is not necessarily done purposely (although recent history shows it can be), but either way it costs you money. The biggest excuse given by customers for not challenging their bank is that the statements are too complicated and they don't understand them. Yes, that is an excuse. You need to make up your mind if you want to waste your money. If you don't, then take your statements to the bank and ask them to explain anything you don't understand – also buy a good financial calculator (I recommend the BA II Plus from Texas Instruments because it's not only a good calculator, it also comes with a very comprehensive instruction manual.) This calculator will help you tackle most financial problems and be able to authoritatively challenge any financial institution. In the final analysis, you have to decide who controls your money – you or your bank. And if you want to be able to exert this control then you need to take a small amount of your time learning how to read and interpret the financial statements sent to you.

Note book: I knew someone who used to key a little notebook and write down every single thing she spent in it. It kind of annoyed me, but later on I figured she might have something. So for one week I carried a little notebook and I wrote down every single penny I spent in cash, with my credit card, or with my chequebook. It was frightening experience I can tell you and it definitely shaved 10 per cent off my spending the second week I did it. While I do not suggest it as a long-term measure, it can have similar effects to smelling salts – it really wakes you up.

Angry, depressed, or hungry: Everyone has heard the advice not to go shopping when you are hungry. But you can add to that depressed or angry. American retail experts have discovered that depressed or angry shoppers spend more than those who are relaxed and happy do when they go shopping.

Banking balances: Many prosperous people never sit down with their bankers and see how they can save money. While banks are not known for handing out free money, they can be helpful. A common problem with many cash rich people is that they keep too much money in low or no interest accounts such as current accounts. A current account is for current expenditure, for money you need in the next month or possibly two. You should move any surplus money into a savings account or other higher-yielding accounts. Many banks now offer a hybrid current account that pays interest on unused balances, but again you might have to request this. So pick up the phone and ask your bank some questions. They should know exactly how much goes into and comes out of your account. Also, ask them what your average cleared credit balance is. This is the average amount of money you have free and clear in your account. If it is substantially above your outgoing you should do something about it. Also if you do have savings, enquire exactly how much you are getting. Just by asking that one simple question the bank employee might immediately suggest a higher interest rate, especially if you suggest you are going elsewhere. On the issue of going elsewhere you might consider 'going offshore' to the Isle of Man or the Channel Islands with your savings. No, they are not just for millionaires or a tax cheat, banking offshore is now accessible to those with as little as £5,000 to invest. There are advantages and disadvantages so discuss it with your bank. Nearly every single Irish and UK bank and building society has a branch in one of the above jurisdictions.

Daily or monthly interest? Ask your mortgage provider how they calculate interest on your mortgage account and it could save you thousands of pounds over the life of your mortgage. Some mortgage providers only adjust the amount you owe them on a yearly basis! This means that all your repayments over the year are not taken off the capital sum until the end of whatever yearly period they use. You are in effect paying interest on money that you have paid them back up to 364 days prior. More progressive mortgage lenders recalculate the amount you owe them on a monthly basis, and some even on a daily basis. There is a chance that all you have to do ask your lender to switch from yearly to monthly, or monthly to daily. Even if they won't facilitate you, if enough individuals ask them then they might bow to the pressure.

Switching mortgages: Switching mortgages is one of those things that can be tantalising and annoying at the same time. By shopping around with different mortgage providers you have a good chance of finding one that will save you money on your monthly mortgage repayment. Then, unfortunately, you have to break the bad news to your current lender who will no doubt have all kinds of obstacles to deter you from changing over. They have your business now and they don't want to lose it, so they aren't going to make it easy for you to leave. Once you have listed the charges that you will incur in changing, you have to decide if it is worth the savings. In the final analysis you are paying a lump sum to make a monthly saving.

Buy quality: Recently two friends of mine both bought washing machines around the same time. The first bought one costing £950, the second spent £250 and thought the other crazy for wasting so much money. However, I still believe my extravagant friend got the better bargain and I can prove it. Firstly, his brand is built to exceptionally high – near professional user – quality. It will last a minimum of fifteen years. My other friend's machine will last him five or six years – if he is lucky. Secondly, the energy and water consumption on the 'expensive' machine is designed to be almost miserly, and this will save the owner between £20 and £25 a year in electricity and water costs compared to standard machines. If we stop here now and look at the per year price of the machines, we will see that my budget minded friend's machine cost him £41 (£250/6 years use). A very good bargain. However, the £950 machine will cost my other friend only £38 per year (£950/15 years minus the £25 energy savings per year over the standard machine). Now this differential is minor, but it still in his favour. You can also add to this other benefits that are hard to quantify financially but are still benefits. The 'expensive' machine can be programmed to switch on at night-time saving more money by using cheaper night-time electricity; it uses less detergent, has a much lower chance of breaking down and incurring expensive repair bills; it spins at 1600 rpm and so removes substantially more water and so requires much less expensive tumble drying. And so on.

So overall, even though one friend initially spent substantially more, the machine is in fact, costing him less per year and hence saving him money. This is reflected in many, but not all aspects of finance; 'money makes money' is an apt expression for this effect. If you have the money in the first place to buy quality, then you will save more money. So when you are buying something, look at factors like the per-year cost and other broad measures rather than just the price you pay at the checkout.

Computer speeds: Most people who go out to buy a computer are attracted to the latest model with fastest CPU speeds, but I am sure they never use these speeds to their fullest potential. If all you are doing is word processing, surfing the net, spreadsheets and the like, then I suggest you might take a computer with 'last year's' speed. It will save you around 20 per cent off the price of the computer and you are unlikely to notice it. If you want to really spend money then take the 20 per cent you saved and buy more memory. Increasing RAM can speed up a computer and provide more flexibility.

Paying by credit card: If you do decide to stick with your plastic then there is one excellent advantage to using it (as long as you pay off the entire balance at the end of the month) that most people do not know about it. Because of strange legal technicalities the credit card company can be held liable for problems you may have with a retailer. So if you pay £500 for an item that breaks down and if you receive no satisfaction from the shop that sold it you then you can pursue your credit card company in certain circumstances. Check with your credit card company for details.

Daily habits: Most people buy a newspaper, a cup of coffee, a soft drink, etc on a frequent basis. Sometimes 'frequent' becomes automatic. Do you really read that daily newspaper or just glance at it? How much does it cost per year? Do you really need those two cappuccinos every day? What appears to be a cheap daily part of life sometimes becomes a large yearly expense. The Italian frothy brew might 'only' cost two pounds a cup (with the lovely little biscuit thrown in for free) but that could be four pounds a day, and twenty pounds a week and a thousand pounds a year. If you had to walk in and pay out one-thousand pounds in cash to your regular coffee house every Jan 1st, would you really do it? Imagine counting out ten, twenty, thirty… Don't get me wrong – I am not questioning buying coffee or going to cafes. That regular cup everyday might be just what you need to unwind, what I am saying is look at your daily routine and ask that question: "It this item really worth it, do I get value from it, or is it just a habit I have developed." Just think about it.

Extended warranties: Extended warranties are becoming a very popular and profitable item for stores. Extended warranties mean that you can purchase a 'guarantee' for your appliance, which extends beyond the normal one-year period. They seem to offer extra assurance and protection but you should question whether the price is worth it for many items. Most modern electronic appliances don't break down that often, and those that do will probably do so in the first year if there is some production flaw in the piece of equipment. My advice is to save the cash and absorb the risk of repair yourself.

Buying a 'fixer upper': A fixer-upper is a second-hand house that needs work in order to bring it up to scratch. Many such homes are great bargains, but many are not. First of all, you should know exactly what you are getting yourself into. What exactly needs fixing? Are you really capable of doing it? People have a romantic idea of doing a bit of painting, laying some nice floor boards and the like. However, I have known couples to buy houses that held more secrets than the CIA. Every time they went to do one thing they exposed more and more problems – problems that were structural in nature and were well beyond their capabilities. There is a movie called *The Money Pit* and I think it should be mandatory viewing for all couples interested in buying fixer-uppers. The wrong house can bury you financially and make coming home from work like starting work all over again. Quantify exactly what you are getting yourself into.

Look for lost money: No, not behind the sofa, but in financial institutions. Recent reports show that banks, building societies, insurance companies, stock brokers and so on, are holding billions that belong to us in dormant accounts of various types. The reasons are numerous, accounts we forgot about, share certificates and policies we lost, changing addresses and not informing people or misplaced documents after the death of a relative. The first step is deciding to search, the second step is doing the search. Both have their own difficulties. People don't search because they don't know they are missing something. To search you must be motivated by something. So you should almost assume that somewhere out there is a financial institution with money belonging to you and it's your job to get it. So how do you get it? Well the best way to start will require about twenty envelopes, twenty stamps and about an hour of your time. Simply take out the yellow pages and find the list of all the large national banks and building societies and their head offices, followed by the list of all the major insurance/assurance companies. Pick the top twenty and send a letter requesting information to each one. In the letter state your full name and address (including any previous ones – very important!), birth date, maiden name and ask the institution to search for any dormant accounts or polices belonging to you. Also if your parents have passed on, include their names (including your mother's maiden name) and all the addresses they lived at. Make the letter brief and to the point. In most cases you can probably do one letter and photocopy it, but do sign it by hand so it doesn't look too much like a 'form letter'. If you think it appropriate, I would also approach the major stockbrokers with a similar letter.

Kids days out: Taking children out these days can be very expensive, and it may seem as though you need to take out a second mortgage. Dedicated theme parks and cinemas are expensive and full of hooks to pull money out of your pocket. Those advertising attractions for kids play on the parents guilt factor and mildly suggest that neglect charges will be pending if you don't bring your off-spring to their attraction. But there are many things to do and places to bring kids that are free, enjoyable, and God forbid, educational. The top three in quick succession are The countryside (the place with the green stuff on the ground), airports (kids love 'em – god knows why), factories (honestly! Many of the larger ones have really interesting guided tours).

Avoid credit cards: It's worth repeating this point again and again. If you spend £2,000 on a credit card with a 20 per cent APR and just make the lowest minimum payments that some now offer (3 per cent of the outstanding balance), then you will pay close to £4,300 before you finally clear that debt; and it will take you *twelve years!!* Most people know what 20 per cent is, they just don't understand the significance of 20 per cent compound interest rates. The biggest cost saving you can make, if you carry a balance, is to get a pair of scissors out and perform a summary execution of your cards.

Garage sales: Garage sales are an American habit but we can all sell off our extra junk via free ad magazines or some such way. Most people have a lot of junk that they don't want to throw out, but which clutters up their homes. It is probably perfectly good, but they have either got something better or don't need it any more. So sell it; it generates cash, but it also frees up space in your home and you might just be able to squeeze the car into the garage.

Conserve petrol: We all know how expensive petrol is but from most of our driving habits, it seems we sometimes forget this. The first important point is to put the right octane level in your car. While 'Super Extra Premium Gold Petrol' sounds great and may give you the impression that it will do wonders for your car, it may not. If you use a higher octane rating than the manufacturer recommends, then you may damage your car.

On the issue of driving habits, there are two important money savers. First, most people think that driving at 55, 65, 75 or 85 mph means that you use the same amount of fuel. After all, it seems logical because you cover the distance faster and hence are burning fuel for a shorter period, so it all probably balances out in the end. Wrong. US government tests have proved that the faster you drive above 60 mph, the lower your fuel efficiency. So if you drive 100 miles at 70 mph and someone else does it at 80 mph, then you will use less fuel. I know, it's a pretty boring and mundane point, but it still saves money so keep your speed around 60 mph on the roads. I might also add that, except for motorways, the speed limit is around 60 mph (there you go, government bureaucrats do think sometimes).

The second point about driving is that those who anticipate traffic cycles save fuel. Just learning how to read the road can save much fuel and wear on your brake pads. Why drive to what you know will be a red light when you can coast? Why accelerate quickly away from lights when you know that two hundred yards down the road there is a round-about. Sorry to be such a killjoy, but that's the way it is.

Look in your bin: Not a very nice experience, I can assure you, but do take a look. Everything in there you paid for, so you are throwing out your own money. A bin contains a wealth of information about your habits and this can save you money. For example, if you have a bin full of expensive paper towels then you might buy a couple of dish clothes and just wash them out. Or if you are constantly using jars of expensive spaghetti sauce then you might consider making your own. It only takes a few minutes, can be stored, and costs a small fraction of the cost of the ready-made sauce you buy in the supermarket. I am not urging self sufficiency, just a little logic in what you buy.

Buy seasonally: It never ceases to amaze me that Christmas cards are sold for 10 or 20 per cent of their cost in January and nobody buys them. Why is this? Christmas is only eleven months away and most people expect to be alive for it, so why not buy and bury the cards in your drawer. This is a small facet of a large problem. Most people buy what is presented on the shelves or racks when, with a little forward planning, there are substantial savings to be made by forward buying. Winter coats in June and swimwear in October cost significantly less but we just don't exploit these bargains. A little forward planning saves a lot. Don't just think about it, do it!

Rechargeable batteries: There are ads on TV for batteries nearly every hour on every channel. These ads are run by battery companies who use stuffed animals, banging drums and various other strange props in a vain attempt to convince us that their batteries last longer than those of competition. Yet there are batteries that last forever, on which no advertising money is wasted but which very few people buy. These are rechargeable batteries, and they are literally money machines.

The major stumbling block, which prevents people from buying them, is the initial hurdle of spending twenty or so pounds buying the actual batteries and the charger. We prevaricate and shudder at the thought and just buy the "regular ones". Yet any initial investment will be saved in just a few months if you use batteries frequently.

Buying a full set of batteries and a high quality re-charger is like buying a money tree. Year after year after year, it will save you money and ensure you always have batteries on hand. The average cost of recharging a set of batteries from the mains is about one to two pence. One or two pence compared with two or three pounds every time you buy alkaline batteries. But people still will not make that initial investment to save. Be smart and do it now. N.B. Don't believe the hype about 'high drain' appliances not being suitable for rechargeable batteries. I have a digital camera with a flash and I use rechargeable batteries. They definitely don't last as long as alkaline, but who cares! It only costs a couple of pence and a few hours to recharge them.

Join a library: Until recently, the last time I was in a public library was when I was fourteen. I had an image of them as stodgy old places full of old ladies and even older books. But this has all changed. They now contain most of the recent up to date best sellers, free internet access, and many helpful con-sumer magazines. When you consider the price of new books, especially hardbacks, it can be quite a saving on your annual reading bill. It is quite funny, but going to the library is an event that has slipped away from many twenty or thirty something's.

Eating on the go: One of the 'busy persons' biggest expense is eating outside the home. But this has three drawbacks. It is expensive, it takes time queuing and the food is usually junk. I found a solution when I saw a very elegant stainless steel 'lunch pail', as the Americans would call it. It contained an oval shaped container for lunch, a small flask with cup, and it had a folding fork. It was basically a very glamorous way to bring a packed lunch. Many people shy away from packed lunches because they think it looks cheap. They are right – it is very cheap and what's wrong with that. But with this lunch set, it also looks stylish. In the average year, if you spend only three pounds a day on some junk, then you are spending close to a thousand pounds. The lunch set cost over £40 but has being earning its keep ever since for me. When I am making a dinner, I usually make a little extra and keep it in the fridge, then every morning I put a large portion in the pail along with some fresh juice and a napkin. The total cost I estimate, is around 30 pence. It tastes good, it takes minutes to prepare and it is relatively healthy. Whether I am in a car, a train, or an office, it is easy, quick and inexpensive. If you are sick of sitting in some supposedly European café waiting for the waitress to bring you a minuscule coffee and even more minuscule sandwich (total cost five pounds) then move up to the lunch pail.

Yearly, versus quarterly payment: Many payments, such as car insurance, can be paid either quarterly or annually. However, sometimes the annual payment is more than four quarterly payments, and this can be quite a bit more. If you can afford it, then make one payment rather than four quarterly or twelve monthly ones. It is the best way to invest your money as you are probably getting a better return than if you left the money in the bank. Remember that convenience and smaller 'packaging' costs you money.

Baby-sitting co-operative: This is an idea I discovered when I lived in the US, and it is real humdinger, as they would say there. A problem faced by many young couples is baby-sitting. Normally they need to find a baby-sitter, pay her and transport her back and forth. The said baby-sitter is usually a sixteen to eighteen year-old female who is more interested in TV and boy-friends (the latter usually arrives after you have left). The solution is to set up a baby-sitting co-operative. Step 1 – Knock on all the doors in your neigh-bourhood or apartment block and locate at least four other young couples and invite them around for a brief chat. Step 2 – Explain to them that you all face the same baby-sitting dilemma so why not baby-sit back and forth for each other. Then someone asks the question "but won't it get very compli-cated keeping track of who is sitting for who and won't some couples do more than others". Yes, they would except for the tokens (this is the "why didn't I think of this" section). Each couple are issued three or four tokens at the beginning, these can be old coins or from a board game, just once they are unique and recognisable. So, if I baby-sit for you one night, then you give me one token (by baby-sit I mean that you bring your child over to me and I take care of it). Then another night I can use that token to 'buy' a night's babysitting from another couple in the circle. They can then use my token with others in the circle, or with me (it grows on you, just wait). Each couple is then free to build up babysitting tokens in a quiet time for them, or to run down their supply in an active period. With each other's phone numbers pasted in front of the phone, it is usually possible to locate another sitter very quickly. Saturday nights out are possible because you will find that one couple may be willing to stay in and mind kids because they might earn more tokens from (a) minding more than one child or (b) charging more than one token. It is a true free market system and balances itself perfectly because as couples run down on tokens they are very eager to baby-sit to build up tokens again for future use. You might even find people ringing you up to offer to baby sit on popular nights. Once the couple-selection process is good and other ground rules are laid out then the system works really well. It is win-win-win. You have competent babysitters, who are 'free' (saving cash), who live nearby (saving more cash on taxi fares), and who aren't your social friends, so it allows you to socialise.

The longer you think about it, the more it does grow on you and the more flexible you realise it is. It is really a microcosm of capitalism with money replaced by more valuable babysitting tokens. Would you be willing to stay in a New Year's Eve night for four or more tokens? Just maybe. In fact a famous American economist uses this system as a 'test bed' for many of his theories on pricing and markets, but that's another story.

Learn to haggle: It essential that you learn to haggle over prices. Some people have serious problems with this and the only way to overcome this fear is to face it. The fear is mostly a fear of embarrassment or a fear of looking 'cheap'. But this fear will cost you money. Most small to medium retailers are open to negotiation about the price simply because they want to stay in business. If a retailer is selling you a TV at £600, then he is probably making around £150 profit and he is unlikely to let that profit walk out the door for the sake of £20 or £30 less. Now obviously there are places for haggling and places not to haggle. If the check-out girl tells you "that will be £63.52 please", then I don't suggest you open negotiations at £60.00. Generally speaking, if there are salespeople on the premises then you can haggle. One big plus for hagglers are credit or charge cards. Most small retailers hate these, especially charge cards, because they can cost them between 2 and 5 per cent service charge and on top of that, they can take over a month to pay the retailer. So just by 'threatening' to use that popular green charge card, you may be able to secure at least 5 per cent off.

Stop the wedding insanity: I risk getting myself in trouble with this one, but I will jump in anyway. Many weddings are nothing but a sinful waste of money by people who can ill afford it. Weddings have moved from romantic/family affairs to events that closely resemble a conveyor belt at an automobile plant. Couples are systematically stripped of cash by an industry that preys on a couple's desire for a "special day." What most get in the end are McWeddings that most of the guests cannot differentiate from the ten or twenty other weddings they have attended. Weddings should be unique and memorable affairs and this can be achieved while also saving money. Saving money is obviously not the primary aim, but it is a win-win situation when you break free from the industrial production line that produces most modern weddings.

While this brief discussion cannot possibly discuss alternative weddings, I have some basic pointers that should stimulate discussion. So ask yourself the following questions. (a) In an ideal world, who would you really invite to your wedding? – Write them down. (b) If you take the orthodox route, who would you *have to* invite? (c) If you held your wedding on a Tuesday, who would come to it? (d) If you got married in Las Vegas, Monaco or Sydney and had ten close friends and a good holiday would you prefer it? (e) Who is running your wedding, you or your parents? (f) If you eloped and returned married would anyone really worry about it in a year? (g) The average full wedding costs between £5,000 and £15,000 which is also the average cost of furnishings for a new house. Are eight or nine hours worth it?

Clocking your calls: Get a stopwatch, small clock, or the like and put it by the phone. When I did this, I cut my bill by over 15 per cent. However, I didn't notice any discernible difference in my calls, I wasn't consciously watching the clock, rushing or timing myself. But I must have done something, because the average call length fell. I presume once we become conscious of time ticking by, then we say what we have to say in a faster fashion. However, it works so try it.

Rent tools: There is a lot to be said for buying items that you use on a continuous basis. It is illogical to continually dribble out money for something you should purchase. However, there is an equally strong argument on the other side that says you should not buy things you don't use that often. Owning something you don't really need means you have to maintain it, repair it, store it and so on. So before you buy a hedge-clippers, floor sander, wall paper stripper or whatever, you should enquire how much it costs to rent one from many of the equipment rental stores that have popped up.

Buy in bulk: Buying in bulk will quite often save money. It never seeks to amaze me that people repeatedly buy small quantities of what they use regularly even when two half litre packs cost much more than a one-litre pack. Buying in bulk is a solid investment of your money as long as you use the item on a continuous basis. And the bigger the better. Try to get into wholesalers markets if you can and buy catering sizes of products, these can save you even more money.

Chapter 11

EMERGENCY ROOM

This chapter is primarily designed to be an addendum or emergency replacement to individual professional financial advice. If you are in serious personal financial jeopardy, then this chapter will help you, but I advise you to also seek the help of a financial planner, accountant or the relevant government organisation which is designed to deal with budgeting and debt for consumers – see Appendix C.

However, I am confident that what I say below cannot make matters any worse, and will more than likely improve your situation dramatically. Most people are embarrassed, or possibly mortified is a better word, by some of the financial messes they find themselves in. This can mean that they are too embarrassed to ask for professional help until it is too late. This is where this chapter comes into its own; nobody will ever know you are reading it, only you.

Next, we should get things into perspective. You may be in financial trouble, you may be up to your neck in debt, you may be feeling embarrassed even humiliated. "What will the neighbours/ relatives/ friends say?" Well the answer to that question requires a trip to your local hospital. Go during visiting hours and just sit with some lonely patients for a while – trust me there are a lot of them. While you are there, you will see many seriously ill people, people who cannot get out of their beds, or even some people who may never get out of them again. So ask yourself a question, "how many of them would trade places with me?" All of your financial problems fade into insignificance when you realise what is facing many other people. So count your blessings and let's try to solve your problems, but just remember you should consider yourself lucky that these are *your* problems. In six months or a year you can have everything behind you.

Now, there are three things we need to do. The first is to get an accurate picture of where you stand at the moment and plot a route out of this current mess, the second is to find out *why* you are in this situation, and the third is to point you permanently in the right direction. While getting yourself out of your current dilemma may seem like your most important goal, it is only really a short-term one. You really have to find out why you ended up in this mess in the first place, otherwise you run the risk of ending up right back up in trouble again quite soon. Also, once you have finished this chapter, you must go back and read this book from the start, assuming you haven't already done so.

The Starting Point

Gather together all of your bills, all of those letters you haven't opened, all your bank and credit card statements, all of your savings books (if any) and so on. In short, you want to sit down at a table with every financial document you have available to you. Open every envelope and stack the documents in one large pile beside you. Get a pen and paper and start writing down each creditor with an amount you owe them. This is going to be tough but do it, you have to arrive at a total figure. Also write down when each amount is due and how urgent the payment is. For example, if the electricity is going to be cut off, then put four stars beside it. If the car is going to be repossessed then maybe that might be three stars. Non-important bills (that must still be paid) might get one or two stars. You yourself should decide how urgent each bill is to you, but focus on the important things. Next, write down the interest rate you are paying on each bill. This may be difficult to find in some cases but if you examine each statement closely you can usually find it. Some bills such as telephone, will not have an interest rate on display so just leave it blank. Finally, write down a contact phone number for each creditor.

You should then total the outstanding amounts and arrive at a total debt figure. It's all right to scream, or cry at this stage, but just remember the people in hospital.

Next, on a separate piece of paper, write down what cash or savings you have at the moment (if any). Finally, write down your monthly/weekly income. You now have an accurate picture of what you owe and what is important. This is reality. This is what you are faced with and there should be no squirming around this issue – it won't change matters at this stage. But it can be dealt with from now on, no matter how bad you think it is, it can be dealt with.

Let's turn the tables and look at things from the point of view of your creditors. You owe them money, they have probably been trying to contact you without success. If they cannot contact you, they get worried about getting their money and so have to jack up the pressure because they assume the worst. They assume you are going to renege on your debts so they take a very offensive posture. However, if they hear from you, then they at least know you haven't skipped the country and abandoned all of your responsibilities. Contacting your creditors is good and it will reduce the pressure on everyone. *So you must communicate with all of your creditors immediately.*

However, in order to communicate with them, you must have something to say, you must have a plan. If you ring up a credit card company and just start waffling on about all manner of things, then this isn't going to get you anywhere. It will make you look weak and indecisive and the company is going to question what kind of person they are dealing with. You must control the situation, and to do this, you must have a debt reduction plan to present to your creditors. I realise that telling you to be 'in control' may seem strange, but the core of many money problems is the lack of control and no matter what your financial situation, you must now learn to exercise control. Ironically, this is as good a time as any, because you have lots of competing people who want your money.

A debt reduction plan is a *clear and credible* plan to reduce your debts rapidly. Look at what cash you have to hand and what income you have and then apportion it over your debts, based on their importance. Deciding who gets what is based on how many stars they have beside them and how willing you think they are to deal with you. Smaller finance companies that you may, for example, be indebted to for your car are more likely to seize it if you offer them a smaller monthly payment than the telephone company will be to cut you off. A rough rule of thumb is that the bigger the organisation, the more willing they are to be flexible because the less important the amount may be to them. This is of course, only a rule of thumb.

Generally, when deciding on monthly payments, you must be realistic and leave yourself enough to live on. When you agree to a repayment plan with your creditors, you want to be able to stick to it. There is nothing worse than getting a creditor to be flexible and then reneging on this. So *be realistic* and not too extreme. You must cut all unnecessary payments and luxuries to the bone and reduce yourself to just the bare minimum living expenses for the time being. I realise that this may be difficult, but in the long-term it will be good for you. For now, realistically estimate your expenses and then decide what you have left to pay.

Stop here now for a moment. You have achieved something important, a big step in the right direction. You have quantified your debts, you have quantified your income and you have figured out how much you have available to pay your creditors. Before you begin to contact your creditors, you should consider a consolidation loan. A consolidation loan is not for everyone but it might just pull you out of the fire. A consolidation loan is a sum in the amount of your outstanding debts which is usually at a lower interest rate and repayable over a longer time-period than your current debts. It allows you to pay off high-interest, short-term debt with a lower longer-term loan; the idea being that the one new monthly payment should be much lower than the sum of all your other payments and hopefully lower than the amount you have calculated that you can afford to repay your creditors. The advantages of a consolidation loan are:

- You can pay off all of your debts and make a fresh start.

- The interest may be tax-deductible.

- You normally pay a much lower interest rate.

- You are spared the difficulty of negotiating with all of your creditors.

- Your credit rating will probably survive intact because you are paying all your creditors off.

If you think a consolidation loan is possible, then you should contact your bank, building society or one of the many institutions that offer such loans. However, *consolidation loans can get you into bigger trouble than you may be in already* so it is important to understand the very high risks and disadvantages you are taking on with such a loan:

- Unless you reform your bad spending habits, you will sink back into debt again, only this time you will have no room to manoeuvre and could face bankruptcy and total financial ruin. If you mess up once, then most financial institutions are willing to be very flexible, but twice is really testing their patience.

- Consolidation loans usually require you to be a home-owner. Although financial institutions may make exceptions, you will find that you are paying a higher rate of interest if the loan is not secured on property. By their very nature, the people who are attracted to consolidation loans are already in trouble and so financial institutions need to get a large tangible asset as security.

- Because consolidation loans are usually secured on your house, then if you don't keep up repayments they may end up costing you your home. Credit card debt will rarely do this. So by going the consolidation option, you may be taking unnecessary risks with your home.

- Consolidation loans also keep you in debt for longer than may be necessary. Scrimping and saving to pay off your debts over the short period may save you a lot more interest payments than being in debt for five or ten years longer.

- Finally, consolidation loans can be seen as too easy an option as they avoid the necessary pain you should feel because of your excesses. This is not a very trendy idea, but nature inflicts suffering on us when we drink or eat too much, stay out in the sun too long, or put our finger on a hot surface. Such discomfort deters us from repeating the activity again, and so it is beneficial to us in the long-term. And so it should be with excessive debt. Tough financial belt tightening and a good dose of embarrassment may be just the kick in the pants we need.

If you have chosen to go the route of the consolidation loan, then you can skip the next section and go to 'retrenchment and reformation'.

With a debt reduction plan in hand, you should now begin contacting your creditors. The first phone call is always the most difficult but it gets easier as you go on. Here's how a phone call might go: Let's say Mary owes *Visa Card* £2,000 and her minimum monthly repayment should be £100. She is going to have difficulty paying this and with 25 per cent interest, she doesn't have a hope of reducing the capital amount if she cannot make the minimum payment. She just faces a cycle of paying interest, on interest on unpaid interest. So she is not only seeking a possible reduction in the minimum payment, but also in the interest rate. Principal must be reduced if you are to get out of debt; otherwise you will be making interest repayments until you are old and grey.

Mary: *Hello can I speak to Mr. Smith in delinquent accounts* (your credit card statements, and others, will almost certainly contain a phone number for people 'in difficulty'.)

Mr. Smith *Hello?*

Mary: *Hello, my name is Mary Jones and my credit card number is xxxx xxxx xxxx xxxx. I have recently encountered some serious financial difficulty but I have embarked on a debt reduction program with the aim of reforming my finances. Your bill is obviously of importance to me so I wish to agree terms to pay off my bill.*

Mr. Smith: *Yes, I see from my computer that your account is in serious arrears, we are going to have to rectify this.*

Mary: *Yes, well my plan is as follows. I can afford to repay £50 per month for the next three months and hopefully when some other debts are out of the way, I can increase this to £75*

Mr. Smith. *Well, I don't know if that will be sufficient as the minimum payment is £100*

Mary: *I realise this, but my finances won't allow this. I haven't been honest with myself recently and have got myself into some short-term financial problems. I'm trying to be honest now and all I can afford is £50, but you are guaranteed to get this every month. I also would like you to decrease the interest rate you are charging me to that of the average term loan (say 10 per cent) and I will of course be returning my Visa card as I have decided that credit cards are not for me at the moment.*

Mr. Smith: *So basically you are asking for 10 per cent interest and £50 per month, hopefully rising to £75?*

Mary: *Yes, and when circumstances permit I will hopefully increase payments above and beyond the £100 figure. I want to get this debt down as soon as possible. I have a stable job, I want to fulfil my obligation to you and make a fresh financial start.*

Mr. Smith: *All right, look I have to clear this with my superior but you sound like a reasonable person who has just gone astray a little. I am sure we can come to suitable terms so we can solve this problem together.*

This may seem utopian but larger financial institutions are willing to be very flexible and deal with customers who they believe are honest and willing to work to solve the problem. And to be honest, many of them have limited choice. Chasing someone for £2,000 worth of credit card debt is a very time consuming, complicated and expensive process – and don't forget this, it is your best lever. Quite often the institutions may sell the debt to a debt collection agency who might give them 50 per cent of the total figure and then only if they collect that amount. They may not collect and the credit-card company has to write off the loss. Any reasonable offer that settles the debt in full will be greeted very eagerly. For this reason, you should realise that asking them to cut the interest rate substantially is no big deal if they are already doubtful about the debt.

Once you have made your first call, you can move on to the rest. Not all will be as easy: some will complain, some may threaten dreadful things, but just tell them that you are attempting to repay, you plan to increase the amount, and that this is the best for both parties that can be achieved. You obviously need to be flexible, but if a non-essential institution refuses to play along with you then you should not become too worried. First, make sure the person on the other end of the phone is able to refuse such an offer. Ask to speak to that person's superior and see if the attitude changes. If it doesn't, then simply write down what happened including the details of your offers to settle the debt and send it by recorded delivery (after you have taken a photocopy, of course). Make whatever payments you have proposed and then see what happens. I am fairly sure they will play ball – what else can they do? Once the repayment plan is somewhat realistic, then I doubt any court would put up with the institution looking for a judgement against you. A genuine and realistic effort to settle a debt is looked upon very favourably by the courts. Just be sure to keep a copy of the letter and the recorded delivery receipt. *It is vital to keep accurate copies of all communications that you have with your creditors.* These include times and dates of phone calls, the people you spoke to and a rough outline of what was said. You should also keep photocopies of all correspondence and send everything recorded delivery.

Once you have reached agreement with some or all of your creditors you will have a big weight lifted from your shoulders. Life will seem different, easier and freer. You will be able to concentrate more of your time on other aspects of your life that had a shadow cast over them. But, and this is the big but, you must now begin the really difficult task of working out why you ended up where you did and then make permanent changes to your life so that you stay back on a straight financial road. This isn't as easy as it sounds. In fact, it is more difficult than negotiating with those you owe money to.

Talking to creditors honestly is easy, the real dilemma is to talk to yourself in a similar fashion. I mean really get inside and have a good look at yourself. The vast majority of people who get into serious debt don't do so because they do not have enough money for medical bills or because they are supporting an elderly relative. Most often they are living beyond their means, and most of the money is frittered away on trinkets and baubles. The real question is why do some people do this, and others do not. Why do some people live wisely and others don't?

First of all dismiss the old excuses, remove them completely from your mind because they will block the real cause. These excuses usually are:

- "I don't earn enough money." Rubbish! Some people live on £5,000 a year so if you have more than £5,000 a year then you are not doing too badly. If you had £50,000 or £100,000 a year then it would probably not be enough either. Bad financial habits consume whatever you earn voraciously.

- "My situation is only temporary, I will be earning more soon and I can catch up then." This is highly unlikely, debt is rarely temporary. It is the result of a problem with controlling your spending. This problem, like bad wine doesn't improve with time.

- "I'm entitled to a few luxuries in life, everyone else has them." Life isn't fair. Repeat this a hundred times and it might sink in. Life isn't fair. Some children get incurable diseases and die, some people are born beautiful and wealthy, some people fall over good luck while others would find the only hole on a twenty acre putting green and fall into it. However, it is also possible to make your own good luck. Hard work, education and saving are within the bounds of most people. Envy is a dead-end street.

- Insert any other excuse you want here. There are many of them and they all skirt around the issues of why people spend too much money.

There are seven questions below and by answering them I think you will discover quite a lot about yourself. It is important to write down the answers. Writing something down is quite different to just thinking about it – I don't know why, but it just is.

Q1 Do you often daydream about winning the lottery? If so, why? What would you change about your life with a few million?

Q2 Do you like spending money?

Q3 Do you envy people with 'lots of money'

Q4 When you buy something non-essential do you think about what it will do for your image?

Q5 What image do have of yourself?

Q6 If your salary doubled or trebled, do you think you would save money?

Q7 Do you think money proves success? If so, why?

The gist of these questions is obvious. Many people, not all, end up in dire straits because they do not fundamentally understand what money is. Money is a means of exchange, it acts as a medium so you can exchange your labour with the labour of others. Before money we had inefficient bartering; Ogg had to meet someone who wanted his newly invented wheel, and who also had lion cloth that he wanted. Such coincidence of wants is rare, so money was invented to lubricate the wheels of commerce. It also helps us to store our labour in the same way generations before stored grain or smoked fish for the winter. Credit, however, allows us to spend labour we have not yet expended.

In many cases, there may be valid reasons for this, but quite often it also allows people to *temporarily* live a lifestyle *they think* they should be living. Some people with low self esteem or a low self image, tend to equate success or failure with the presence or absence of wealth. This is extremely flawed thinking. The path that I suggest should be followed, is work, happiness about that work, positive self image and then monetary reward (large or small). Many of those who get in over their heads are sometimes trying to short-circuit this equation. They think monetary rewards (by way of credit) will work backwards and bring a positive self image and make them happy in their work, relationships or life in general. This is skewed thinking which usually leads to financial mess.

Correcting it is fairly simple. It involves the old basics: hard work, educating yourself, making the tough choices, getting up early to exercise, reading a book instead of watching a video, walking instead of driving, eating home-made instead of pre-packed foods, saving for purchases instead of borrowing for them, eating less fat and more fibre, climbing the stairs instead of taking the lift, using money instead of plastic, and so on. All boring basics that your mother probably told you, but you know the hard way is sometimes the best. Deep down everyone really knows the crux of their own financial messes and if you have started at this chapter, then I suggest you go back to chapter one and begin the book.

A Final Note

You may have noticed that I didn't suggest you make a household or personal budget. This is because I don't really think they work. Budgets can be like diets in the sense that they are 'all or nothing' options. If you break it once or twice it can lead to you abandoning it. It is better to realise that you have problems, rectify these problems, and learn new habits in the process. This should not preclude you from listing monthly expenses so that you are aware of them, or even tracking your spending closely. But a budget in the sense that you have x amount of money to spend and you worship this figure is, I feel, unhelpful.

However, the above is just my opinion: if you think a budget is helpful (and they may very well be for many people) then make a budget. And the simpler the better. Figure out your income, assess how much you need for essentials, how much you need to set aside for irregular payments and saving and then you are left with the amount you can spend on yourself. If need be you should keep the money in cash and only use cash in order to control yourself. You cannot physically spend cash you don't have.

Appendix A

STRESS CONTROL

Stress is one of those things that needs to be experienced in order to fully understand it. I would presume no one reading this hasn't experienced it in some form. It is a difficult to define precisely, but I will try so briefly.

Stress is like being forced to reach beyond our grasp, but the object we are being forced to reach for appears to move further away from us the more we stretch to grasp it. And yet we are pressured to still try to reach it. Stress is not competition, competition is good. The more we strive for that little bit extra, the better we become. Working hard is not stress, working hard can lead to enjoyment and self-improvement. Stress, I believe, differs from hard work and the competitive instinct to achieve because the pressure is coming from outside of ourselves and we feel that we do not fully control the important environmental factors necessary to achieve whatever level we have to.

I like to play the piano. When I start to learn a new piece, I play it horrendously (not that the finished product is much better) but I do improve as I practice. The more I practice, the better I become and, most importantly, I realise this fact. I know that all the factors connected with how I play the piece are within my grasp. If for example, the piano was out of tune and getting worse by the minute, yet I was obliged to play the piece perfectly within 30 minutes, then I think I would start to become stressed.

Stress reduces the quality of life, reduces our capacity to make rational decisions, and can ultimately shorten our lives. Never doubt that stress can and does kill. Stress usually builds up slowly over months, if not years. For example, living in a city environment can be stressful. One source of stress is the constant fight for space of all kinds. Space on the roads, space in elevators, space in cafés, space to park your car, space to eat, space on a hot sweaty underground or bus; just space. It has been shown that white mice go insane when subjected to such space deprivation - and a trip to New York will confirm the strong link between those mice and humans. Pulling humans the other way is the demand for swiftness and speed imposed on us by a busy society. You may be stuck in traffic and sweating, but you have to be somewhere important by 15.00. At 14.45 you are on your mobile making promises you cannot keep. At 15.00 your blood pressure is rising and you start abusing the other drivers who probably cannot hear you anyway. At 15.15 you have reached a clear patch of road and are accelerating towards your destination while dialling the number to confirm that you will now be arriving soon. Then you refocus your eyes on the road only to realise that the cars have stopped again, and after the screeching of brakes and trail of rubber you come to a stop within inches of the stationary bumper in front of you. And so the day goes on. The computer, no matter how fast, isn't fast enough. That printer cannot print fast enough, that connection isn't fast enough, that file will just not transfer fast enough; nothing is fast enough when you are behind schedule and under pressure. This type of long-term pressure builds up slowly until your capacity to function efficiently is reduced. Hopefully, weekends and holidays can unwind you sufficiently so you can carry on, but sometimes weekends and holidays add to the stress.

There are many other varieties of stresses but all have the same consequence, i.e. a reduction in our efficiency and our quality of life. The solutions are simple to quote, but sometimes tricky to implement. I will give you ten sure-fire methods of eliminating and controlling stress that others and I have reported as being great stress-busters.

(1) Exercise:[1] There is no two ways about it, exercise reduces stress. Exercise gets the heart beating overtime, the lungs working to full capacity and generally the body becomes active and alive. The effects of exercise will wash away most immediate stress symptoms.

(2) Stretch: If you cannot go and run around the park or cycle five miles then you should still try to get your body stretching. Yoga has some excellent and simple exercises that can do wonders for the stressed body. Many of these can be done in confined spaces, or even in the car. Two good books on yoga that I can recommend are Judith Lasater's Relax and Renew: Restful Yoga for Stressful Times and Desktop Yoga by Julie T. Lusk.

(3) Relax: Relaxing doesn't necessarily mean lying down and watching TV. Relaxing means doing something you like doing and over which you have control. It might be reading a book, it might be bee-keeping, and it may be sitting in front of the TV watching two teams fight over a leather ball.

(4) Laugh: 'Laughter is the best medicine' and it is also a great stress reliever. If your circumstances don't allow you to laugh, then go see a good comedy or rent out one of those perennially funny Marx Brothers movies. It can't hurt.

(5) Sleep: Eight hours is necessary for most people. Eight hours of good restful sleep without alcohol or other substances to disturb the replenishing of the body. Eight hours of consistent sleep every night of the week will do wonders for stress. Just try it, it's free and enjoyable. This may

---

1. Just to cover myself, you should consult your GP before embarking no any rigorous exercise programme. If you weigh 20 stone and haven't risen from your sofa in ten years, then suddenly trying to become Superman could kill you.

seem a flippant comment, but sleep deprivation is a major problem in our society.

The first five points addressed combating the symptoms of stress, and the next five points suggest how to tackle the causes. And this is where it can be difficult.

(6) Organise: Like many aspects of personal finance, it is obvious that many stressful situations are avoidable if only people organised. Take a simple example: how many people cannot find their cars keys on a regular basis. This minor annoyance can lead to delays that snowball into stressful experiences. That person is to blame and no one else. Everything has a place, and there is a place for everything. A small key rack beside the front door will solve this, and people can extrapolate this forward into all areas of their life.

(7) Eliminate: There used to be people known as time & motion men who went to factories and studied how people worked and suggested how the tasks could be accomplished in a shorter time. Today they are called ergonomic engineers and we can learn much from them. Study your daily routine both at home and at work. Why do you do something the way you do? Can two tasks be combined into one or can tasks even be eliminated completely? Is there a machine that can remove a burden from you? Generally speaking, what changes can be made to remove weights from your shoulders.

(8) Control: Identify the stresses in your life. Write the list down now. The list could include everything from boss to baby or from traffic to travelling. Now begin to identify ways you can deal with each one. This may include just sitting down and talking to the person or working out alternative means of transport. In a study in the US, it was discovered that simply writing down what stresses people felt in the morning reduced the feeling of stress felt during the day.

(9) Help: Sometimes we cannot solve all of our problems on our own and professional help is needed. If you are drowning, then reach out for help. An enlightened GP is a good place to start or possibly a stress councillor.

(10) Removal: If your job is so stressful, then consider the big step of removing yourself from the stressful situation. It may be a big jump, but if you do not like doing what you do, then change. No matter what age you are or what stage you are in your career, consider changing to something else. It is easy to say, but it is not impossible to achieve.

I won't even claim that this brief discussion will solve stress problems which readers have. It should, however, alert you to the possible avenues of self or professional help.

GIVING UP: THE EASY WAY

In case anyone is wondering why a section on giving up smoking is located in a personal finance book, then they should be reminded of the cost. Aside from the obvious health issues, smoking costs you thousands of pounds every year. You buy the damn things, smoking drives up your health and life insurance bills, and you are also at higher risk from damaging your property with cigarette ends. Smoking is about wasting money, your money. So if you can stop, then it's win-win-win for you and you can start saving serious amounts of money.

Quitting smoking by going cold turkey doesn't work very well. How do I know this? Because many other smokers, and I, have tried this way and failed. Quitting cold turkey is like jumping out of bed into an ice cold plunge pool. It is very severe, harsh and presents an all or nothing scenario to the smoker. The only other option to non-smoking is then seen as smoking, so if the smoker can't stop completely, they fall back into smoking full time. Over the years, I knew many smokers, myself included, who alternated from smoking, to not smoking and back again, never really giving up. This absolutist attitude to smoking is constantly reinforced by zealous anti-smoking cliques who have a Stalinist view on tobacco and who really don't help many smokers to quit. In fact in the US, the country with the most rigid anti-smoking laws (and zealots), there has been no significant decline in smoking over the last ten years (in fact studies have shown it is rising in some segments of the population.)

The system that worked for me takes about a year, yes a year, but it has a high success rate and in the end people voluntarily give up cigarettes and don't want to return to them. It is a slow way to give up cigarettes but if it works, who cares – better to have stopped smoking for good in a year than be again off again for the rest of your (shortened) life. So here it goes.

Let's assume you smoke x cigarettes a day. It could be ten, twenty or forty. How much easier for you would it be to smoke x minus one? 'Very easy' would be the reply, what's the difference between twenty and nineteen, very little. And this is the root of the system. First, decide how many you smoke, let's say it is twenty, so x=twenty. Now get a small plastic box and put it in your car or house or office. Next every time you buy a packet of twenty (and for the first week) take one cigarette out and put it in this plastic storage box. So for the first week, you are smoking nineteen and you guessed it, the second week every time you buy a packet of cigarettes you put two into the lunchbox. The only reason I am keeping the cigarettes in the box is to save money, you could throw the cigarettes away but this is a waste. Using this method, you gradually work down to seventeen, sixteen, fifteen, and so on. As the weeks go by, you slowly smoke less. As your lunchbox fills up you can fill up the odd pack with the appropriate number of cigarettes on that day. If you want to resist temptation, you can dispose of the lunch box angle and just chuck the extra cigarettes in the bin every day; it's up to you.

Anyway, the beauty of this system is that you are never faced with the thought of 'never having another cigarette' you just have to have one less each day, and most people have enough will-power to wait until after lunch or for another hour or whatever. The hold-out period is manageable, whereas with the cold-turkey method, the hold out period is infinity. By the time you hit ten a week it may be becoming difficult, but at least you know you *will* have another cigarette. Those of you with a good eye for figures will recognise that I said a year and if I only smoke twenty then I would be down to 1 cigarette after twenty weeks. But it isn't as easy as that. At some stage, it may be ten or five or whenever you will hit a difficult patch. So here you plateau for a few weeks. You might say, I would have ten cigarettes a day for two or three weeks. You will still diligently carry a packet around every day with ten cigarettes in it. But after the two or three weeks start to work down again. You might plateau a few times but do shift down after two or three weeks.

The funny thing is that it becomes easier and easier to give up each cigarette until the reach the final phase. The final phase is what I call the dining and drinking phase. Smokers, and I presume only smokers have made it this far, know that most pleasurable cigarettes are those you have after a meal and with a drink (with one possible exception but we will leave that aside). As your daily intake falls to three or four cigarettes, you will reach a point where you may only be having a cigarette after each meal or drink. At this point you have to jump to a weekly cigarette allowance. Instead of saying "I am going to have three cigarettes a day", you shift down and say "I am only going to have fifteen cigarettes a week".

At this point, your cravings will be reduced to the point that each cigarette will be enjoyed so much you may want to 'save them up' for the weekend. And miraculously, you will find yourself one day going without cigarettes for the whole day so that you can have extra ones on another day. This skipping of a day is the biggest leap, and once you have made this jump you are very close to giving up cigarettes altogether. I arrived at the situation where I allowed myself ten cigarettes a week, all of which I smoked when I went out. I was stuck at this stage for almost six months and then one weekend I just didn't have any. I didn't plan it, it just happened. I knew I could have one, but I just didn't. The next weekend I had about five, and then a break of about of month and another few. It was just a petering out of the habit. It was totally voluntary, and so what if it took a year, I did it and so can you.

Now it may happen that you get stuck at the 'ten a week' plateau for a year, or two years, or even forever. But who cares? Ten cigarettes a week is a lot better than 140, and some day you will stop. There is no need to be overly zealous about matters, you will be saving 90 per cent of your cigarette money and the effects on your health will be drastically reduced. Ten per cent may not be 0 per cent but it is a lot better than 100 per cent.

Appendix C

CONTACTS

If you are in serious financial trouble then you should seek professional advice as well as reading this book. If you do not know where to turn, in Ireland you can contact Money Advice and Budgeting Service on (01) 230 2002, (01) 670 6555. In the UK you can contact your local office of the Citizens Advice Bureau. Both of these organisations are government run, free, and offer excellent services. They will listen to you without being judgmental and if they cannot help you, then they probably know who can.

This book is not designed to replace specific financial advice so if you think you need this you should contact a professional financial adviser. Finding a good adviser is like finding a good dentist – it can be difficult, costly and painful without knowing where to start. The best place to start in the UK is the Institute of Financial Planners (0117) 945 2470 or The Society of Financial Advisers (0181) 989 8464. In Ireland you are best advised to seek out a financial adviser via recommendations by friends or ideally your local bank manager. However, it is important to understand that advisers can be paid in one of two ways; by commission or by some form of hourly rate. Those paid by commission receive money from institutions in which they invest your money. Needless to say this can lead some advisers 'astray'. However, hourly rates for advice can run between fifty and one-hundred pounds, so a good rule of thumb is that if you are seeking advice with small amounts of money then you are better off with a commission based adviser. Once you can ensure they aren't steering you towards the highest commission that is. Alternatively, if you have a large amount of money to invest then go for the hourly rate *and ensure that the adviser refunds you the commission he will receive from any institution.*

Recommended Reading List

Below is a variety of books on finance that I suggest you read in order to obtain specific advice.

- "Which?" Way to Buy, Sell and Move House – by Alison Barr and Richard Barr (Which? Books) ISBN 0852027672. In fact any of the "Which?" series of books are highly recommended – they cover a wide variety of financial topics.

- The TAB [yearly] Guide to Money Pensions and Taxes by Sandra Gannon and Sebastian Devlin (Taxation Institute). Irish taxation and pension guide.

- The Daily Mail Income Tax Guide [yearly] by Kenneth Tingley (Orion Business). This is one of the many 'income tax guides' that are published every year. They are inexpensive and usually very helpful.

- The Motley Fool UK Investment Guide by David Berger, David Gardner and Tom Gardner (Boxtree) ISBN 0752224395. A superb, if slightly irreverent, book on investing, buy this before you consult any financial adviser and you may save yourself a lot of money.

BIBLIOGRAPHY

Bonnie Runyan McCullough, *Bonnie's Household Budget Book* (New York: St.Martin's Griffin) 1981.

Ann Fox Chodakowski & Susan Fox Wood, *Living On A Shoestring* (New York: Dell Publishing) 1997.

James D. Dean, *Breaking Out Of Plastic Prison* (Grand Rapids: Baker Books House Company) 1997.

Mary Hunt, *The Cheap-Skate Money Makeover* (New York: St. Martin's Paperback) 1995.

Andrew Feinberg, *Downsize Your Debt* (New York: Penguin Books) 1993.